Advance praise for *Ten*

Many call the ten Commandments nothing more than archaic rocks that lack relevance in today's modern society. In her fantastic new book *Ten: How the Commandments Can Change Your Life,* Mary Elizabeth Sperry gives these timeless treasures a twenty-first century update, underscoring eloquently and with great relevance how the Commandments remain not only relevant, but indeed essential for any spiritual seeker. More than simply preaching at her reader, Sperry invites us into true connection with these timeless precepts. "Ten" is a compelling guide that deserves to be spotlighted, savored and shared.

—Lisa M. Hendey, author of *A Book of Saints for Catholic Moms* and founder of CatholicMom.com

Mary Sperry's newest book is a robust reflection on the Ten Commandments that is contemplative, energetic. Sperry's tone is almost casual, however, as she encourages, explains, and integrates scripture, saints, people, stories, popular culture and catechism so that you think you are with friends having coffee. Her understanding that living the Commandments is what sustains out relationship with God *and* one another opens the metaphorical door to that grace-filled dimension of life in the Spirit for anyone who has wondered what comes next once he or she obeys the rules.

—Sister Rose Pacatte, FSP, award-winning coauthor of *Lights, Camera, Faith: The Ten Commandments*

A truly good teacher, like the rabbi Jesus, upends your expectations and takes things you thought you knew already and makes you see them new. Mary Elizabeth Sperry knows that trick. With each commandment, she takes you down a path that leads to more interesting, even startling, insights than you could have anticipated. Few writers can put their oral voice on paper. But when Sperry writes in her lively, humorous style you hear the immediacy and vibrant energy of an accomplished speaker. Highly readable is good, but highly useable is better. And this book is both. It's guaranteed to take you on a journey through your soul—and chances are good you'll come out better on the other side.

—Graziano Marcheschi, MA, D.Min., Executive Director of University Ministry Saint Xavier University Chicago

TEN

Love is the fulfillment of the law.
Romans 13:10

Mary Elizabeth Sperry
Christmas 2021

TEN

HOW
THE
COMMANDMENTS
CAN
CHANGE
YOUR
LIFE

MARY ELIZABETH SPERRY

Franciscan
MEDIA
Cincinnati, Ohio

Excerpts from the *New American Bible, revised edition* © 2010, 1991, 1986, 1970
Confraternity of Christian Doctrine, Inc., Washington, D.C. Used with permission.
All rights reserved. No part of this work may be reproduced or transmitted in any form or
by any means, electronic or mechanical, including photocopying, recording, or by any
information storage and retrieval system, without permission in writing
from the copyright owner.

Excerpts from the *Catechism of the Catholic Church, second edition*
© 2001 United States Conference of Catholic Bishops—
Libreria Editrice Vaticana. Used with permission.

Cover and book design by Mark Sullivan
Cover image © Veer | javarman

LIBRARY OF CONGRESS CATALOGING-IN-PUBLICATION DATA
Sperry, Mary Elizabeth.
Ten : how the commandments can change your life / Mary Elizabeth Sperry.
     p. cm.
ISBN 978-1-61636-408-3 (alk. paper)
1. Ten commandments. 2. Catholic Church—Doctrines. I. Title.
BV4655.S64 2012
241.5'2—dc23
                          2012018206
ISBN 978-1-61636-408-3

Published by Franciscan Media
28 W. Liberty St.
Cincinnati, OH 45202
www.FranciscanMedia.org

Printed in the United States of America.
Printed on acid-free paper.
12 13 14 15 16   5 4 3 2 1

For my godparents,

Robert Kontur

(rest in peace)

and

Carol Lee Regets Gagliardi

Then God spoke all these words:

I am the Lord your God, who brought you out of the land of Egypt, out of the house of slavery. You shall not have other gods beside me.

You shall not make for yourself an idol or a likeness of anything in the heavens above or on the earth below or in the waters beneath the earth; you shall not bow down before them or serve them. For I, the Lord, your God, am a jealous God, inflicting punishment for their ancestors' wickedness on the children of those who hate me, down to the third and fourth generation; but showing love down to the thousandth generation of those who love me and keep my commandments.

You shall not invoke the name of the Lord, your God, in vain. For the Lord will not leave unpunished anyone who invokes his name in vain. Remember the sabbath day—keep it holy. Six days you may labor and do all your work, but the seventh day is a sabbath of the Lord your God. You shall not do any work, either you, your son or your daughter, your male or female slave, your work animal, or the resident alien within your gates. For in six days the Lord made the heavens and the earth, the sea and all that is in them; but on the seventh day he rested. That is why the LORD has blessed the sabbath day and made it holy.

Honor your father and your mother, that you may have a long life in the land the LORD your God is giving you.

You shall not kill.

You shall not commit adultery.

You shall not steal.

You shall not bear false witness against your neighbor.

You shall not covet your neighbor's house. You shall not covet your neighbor's wife, his male or female slave, his ox or donkey, or anything that belongs to your neighbor.

—Exodus 20:1–17

CONTENTS

ACKNOWLEDGMENTS

No author can claim sole credit for any book. Moving a book from an idea to a published product requires the efforts of many people. I'd like to thank a few who helped make this book a reality.

First thanks must go to the wonderful Lisa Biedenbach and Mary Carol Kendzia of Franciscan Media. They came to me with the idea for this book and gently guided me throughout the writing process, sharing insights and offering encouragement. And they never thought it was strange to talk me through writer's block on Facebook!

Thank you to my supervisors at the USCCB, Paul Henderson and Helen Osman, who made it possible for me to write this book.

It takes a village to raise a child, but it takes a neighborhood to keep me on task, so I'd like to thank my wonderful neighbors who always asked about the book and encouraged me when I didn't think I'd finish: Vicki, Leta, Josh, Cathy, Eva, Sayre, Chris, and Edwin.

Special thanks to my friends who listened to me complain and let me clarify my ideas, especially Noreen (my volunteer agent!), Lisa, Steve, Greg, Gabino, and Jennifer. Extra special thanks to Rae Ann who actually read the entire thing and gave me great advice.

Thanks to my dog, Hershey, who proved definitively that it is possible to write an entire book with a dog asleep on your chest.

My sisters, Kathy and Carol Ann, gave their support throughout the writing process.

Nothing I have accomplished in my life would have been possible without the love and support of my parents, Katherine and William. I love you even more than you know.

Most of us likely learned the Ten Commandments very early in our lives, and many may have misinterpreted them as a checklist of what to do and not to do. In *Ten,* Mary Sperry explores these ten "words" of Deuteronomy not so much as a checklist of right and wrong, but as they truly are: a response of love from a loving and gracious Father whose words of love become incarnate in the Word made flesh, Jesus Christ.

As the *Catechism of the Catholic Church* points out, the Decalogue (ten words) forms a coherent whole , each referring to the others and so are to be seen as one loving response. The author provides good rationale as to why the Decalogue survived to guide followers of Jesus when the dietary laws of the Old Testament did not.

Easy to read and filled with practical suggestions, each chapter of this book explores the depth of each commandment. In the end what is reinforced is the priority of honoring God first and then our neighbor, as the author guides the reader in to discovering that the priority of God in our lives is vital to being able to enter into right relationships that ensure that we will love people and use things rather than the opposite.

While it can be tempting to treat the commandments as almost a self-help manual and fall victim to the ancient heresy that marred the life of the fourth-century monk Pelagius of "earning salvation," this treatment portrays God's grace in our response to our loving God. The emphasis is on the action of God in our hearts that brings about the internalizing of these precious ten words so that good and faithful habits result. On a personal note, I have had the privilege to know the author and have seen her admirable efforts to live what she presents in writing.

Most Reverend Joseph E. Kurtz, D.D.
Archbishop of Louisville

Habits for Right Relationships

The Ten Commandments. The very words conjure up memories of the booming, majestic voice of God and ancient laws engraved on stone tablets while Moses stood on Mount Sinai. But what can they possibly have to say to us? We live in a digital world; stone tablets are things we see in museums (or in photos on the Internet that we access from our *real* tablets). How can these commandments apply to us? It's not like we're going to go out and commit murder or armed robbery. It's easy to see the Ten Commandments as outdated, legalistic, not meaningful to us.

Before we can think about how the Ten Commandments apply to us, we need to take a look back.

God gave Moses the Ten Commandments in the chaotic and frightening days after the Israelites escaped slavery in Egypt. The Israelites had witnessed God's power, from the plagues to the parting of the Red Sea to the provision of food and water in the desert. Despite these powerful signs, they had to be troubled, anxious, and frightened. The Israelites had lived in Egypt for generations, so they had to abandon everything they knew, facing the unknown dangers and hardships of a journey through the desert—a journey that would ultimately take forty years.

In this uncertain time, God was their rock—the only certainty they knew—always present before them in a pillar of cloud or of fire. And this powerful, ever-present God was making them an offer they couldn't refuse. He offered them a relationship with him: they would be his people and he would be their God. The Ten Commandments, chief among the laws of the covenant, established the Israelites' responsibilities in this relationship. God promised to be present to protect and care for his people. In return, the children of Israel promised to live by these commandments. (The rest of the Old Testament relates the story of the Israelites' successes and failures in living by the commandments and God's unfailing love in response.)

It's a nice story (and it made a great movie), but what does it have to do with us? After all, we don't obey the rest of the laws given to Moses. In fact, some of those laws, such as those regarding the appropriate management of slaves, we find offensive today. What's special about these ten? Why are they still in force?

Nearly two thousand years after God gave them to Moses on Mount Sinai, the Ten Commandments were still a topic of study and discussion. A scholar of the law tested Jesus, asking him to name the greatest of the commandments—sort of a pop quiz. Jesus answered the scholar's question by summarizing the commandments: "You shall love the Lord, your God, with all your heart, with all your soul, and with all your mind. This is the greatest and the first commandment. The second is like it: You shall love your neighbor as yourself. The whole law and the prophets depend on these two commandments" (Matthew 22:37–40).

In Jesus's summary, we find the reason why these commandments are still meaningful for us today. These commandments remain important because they teach us how we should relate to God, self, others, and things. When our relationships are healthy and ordered appropriately, our lives are in balance. We know a joy that goes beyond momentary, fleeting pleasure. We are surrounded by love. We live our call to holiness.

Let's look more closely at Jesus's summary. Jesus established clear priorities for our relationships. The most important relationship (and the foundation of all other relationships) is love of God. If we love God entirely—with our whole heart and mind and strength and soul—we will have more, not less, love to give to others.

Second, we must attend to our relationship with ourselves. If we are to love our neighbors as ourselves, we must have a healthy love of self. The person who does not love himself or herself will not truly love his or her neighbors. Self-love doesn't mean that we are selfish or arrogant. It requires that we recognize our intrinsic value as loved children of God. As children of God, we are precious and worthy of dignity and love.

A healthy self-love is the ground for our love of neighbor. The person who truly understands himself or herself as a child of God cannot help but extend that understanding to others. Building on this under-standing, we will choose ways of living that show care for others, those close to us and those we do not know. We will judge our actions by their impact on others rather than by their convenience or personal benefit. We will give of ourselves wholeheartedly, without reservation.

But we cannot turn our attention from Jesus's summary without looking at what is left unsaid. Nowhere in his summary of the greatest commandments does Jesus mention possessions. Our relationship to things must take a backseat to the three relationships Jesus mentions: God, self, and others. Things will never be as important as God or people. In fact, several times during his ministry on earth, Jesus makes it very clear that relying on possessions is a futile pursuit. No matter how much easier or pleasurable things can make our lives, they can never substitute for a healthy relationship with God, self, or others. If our possessions become the focal point of our lives, our relationships will be out of balance.

We live in a culture where self-help is practically a religion. Bookstores have entire sections devoted to books that help us plan our finances, get in shape, and control our addictions to food, approval, sex, or shopping. Turning on the television introduces the ideas of the latest minted expert on life, filling an ever-expanding media universe. Websites teach us how to have a clean house, a perfect marriage, and a well-balanced retirement portfolio. You can download apps to count your calories, keep track of your finances, and plan your exercise.

All of these resources are really about the same thing: helping us to develop the right relationships in our lives—making sure that the things that really matter get our attention. But is it possible the answer has been here all the time? Isn't this, in fact, what the Ten Commandments do?

Our lives are constructed by the choices we make and do not make, by what we do and by what we do not do. Choosing the same way over a period of time creates a habit. For example, if I choose, day in and day out, to eat fresh fruit as a snack instead of potato chips or to climb the steps instead of using the elevator, in a matter of weeks, I will have developed a habit that will make me healthier and help me get into better shape. On the other hand, if I work out only when I feel like it or eat properly occasionally, my inconsistent choices will never become a habit.

The Ten Commandments teach us habits that we need to develop to live in right relationship with God, self, others, and things. They help us to live more intentionally in the relationships that mark a healthy and holy life. With the Ten Commandments as our guide, our choices will help us develop habits that make our relationships healthy and balanced. We will develop habits that help us grow in wholeness and holiness.

The Ten Commandments are guideposts; they help us to make the right choices and develop the habits that lead to healthy relationships. These habits don't mean that our lives and relationships will be perfect and without difficulties. Without question, we will experience setbacks and trouble. And sometimes we'll fail, doing what is easy rather than what is right. But through it all, the Ten Commandments, and the habits they teach, will act as a spiritual GPS, helping us recalculate when we get off the path and redirecting us on to the path of wholeness and holiness.

How to Use This Book

This book isn't a theological tract or a devotional. You might think of it as a workbook to help you develop the spiritual habits that will lead you to a better relationship with God. As such, it's not really the sort of book you should read in a single sitting, moving from chapter to chapter. Developing new habits takes time. We don't develop bad habits overnight and we won't replace them with good habits overnight.

I recommend reading this book one chapter at a time, taking time after each chapter to do the journaling exercises and to examine the way you follow (or don't follow) each commandment. The chapters build on each other, so it's important to go in order. Move to the next commandment when you feel ready to move forward. Feel free to go back to earlier chapters when things begin to feel out of balance. You might also want to keep this book on your shelf for a while, returning to it occasionally (perhaps each Lent) as a checkup on your spiritual development or as a refresher course to help deepen your relationship with God.

Points to Remember

- Jesus summarized the Ten Commandments when he gave the Two Great Commandments: "You shall love the Lord, your God, with all your heart, with all your soul, and with all your mind. This is the greatest and the first commandment. The second is like it: You shall love your neighbor as yourself. The whole law and the prophets depend on these two commandments" (Matthew 22:37–40).
- Our lives are formed by the choices we make. We can choose to do what is right or to do what is easy. Over time, those choices will determine the path of our life.
- The Ten Commandments help us to make the right choices, leading us to right relationships in all aspects of our lives.

Try This

For a week, spend a few minutes before bed thinking through your day and answering the following questions, writing your answers in a journal:

- What parts of your life feel out of balance?
- What concerns or relationships take the majority of your time and energy?
- What activities and relationships give you energy?

At the end of the week, review all the entries and see what patterns become obvious. As you read the chapters about each of the commandments, identify which commandments might underlie the imbalances you see.

Talk It Through

- When and how did I learn about the Ten Commandments?
- What would healthy (not perfect) relationships look like?
- How do I make moral decisions? What are my guides?

Pray

God,

sometimes my life gets crazy and out of control.

It seems to be more than I can handle.

Please give me your light and your help

to get through the confusion

and find the path that leads to happiness in you.

Amen.

CHAPTER ONE

THE FIRST COMMANDMENT
Creating Priority

I, the LORD, am your God.
You shall not have strange gods before me.

The first commandment seems pretty straightforward. There is one God—no more, no less—and we need to worship that one God. No photocopies or facsimiles accepted. Not a lot of room for confusion there. Yet, from the beginning, it has been a problem for people. Moses wasn't even all the way down Mount Sinai before the Israelites were worshiping a golden calf as their god. Despite seeing God's power displayed in the plagues, the parting of the Red Sea, and the provision of food and water in the desert, doubt and fear had crept in, clouding their judgment.

This commandment is still a challenge, even though it seems foreign to modern ears. Unlike the ancient Israelites, very few of us are likely to be tempted to offer sacrifice to golden calves or other pagan gods—unless we call those gods by their more common names: power, wealth, approval, fame. Every day people offer up their time, energy, and money at those modern altars. The first commandment requires that we offer worship only to the one true God, made incarnate in Jesus Christ and revealed in the Holy Spirit. Following the faith of the Church allows us to know that we are faithful to this one true God. In a culture where cynicism is prized as a virtue, living in this faith may be harder than it seems. Atheism or a vague belief in a Supreme Being who has little contact with and makes no requirements of human beings goes against this commandment.

Some people may see this commandment as overly harsh, condemning the doubt and faith struggles that mark the lives of even the holiest of people. Believing is hard work. Everyone has doubts and periods when it's hard to keep the faith. What matters is how you respond to these experiences. Doubt, if persistently fostered and entertained, can be a danger, leading us away from God. However, feeling that your faith is being tested or strained, especially in times of great difficulty, is well-documented in the lives of the saints. The struggle to maintain faith through difficulties may, ultimately, lead to a stronger and deeper faith.

But keeping the first commandment is not as simple as avoiding atheism or not entertaining beliefs that deny the truths of faith. Quite simply, this commandment reminds us that God must be our ultimate priority. No relationship, no desire, no achievement, no other good may take precedence over God. When we allow anything, no matter how good it may seem, to become more important than God, our relationships become unbalanced, and we need, once again, to find the right path.

Priorities, Priorities

Setting priorities is an essential task in life, true for individuals and businesses, governments and organizations. No individual or entity has unlimited resources. Even the extremely wealthy face limits of time, attention, and energy. Since resources are always limited, you have to decide what is important enough to make a claim on them. We simply can't do everything we'd like to do. We just can't. That means that we have to decide what activities, interests, and relationships will have the first claim on our limited resources.

That decision-making takes a variety of forms. Democratic governments hold elections, in part, to decide which set of competing priorities will take precedence. Businesses may hire planning experts to help them identify priorities and organize their structures and processes to pursue their priority goals. Some individuals seek out counselors or life coaches to help them sort through the competing priorities in their lives.

The first commandment reminds people of faith that their first priority must always be their relationship with God. Without centering our priorities first and foremost on God, we spend our time and energy pursuing things that will give us momentary pleasure or comfort, but not the true, lasting joy and peace that we seek. When God is our ultimate priority, our other priorities will fall into place. Putting God first makes claims on our time and energy. If God is first and we truly seek to follow his will, our obligations are not fulfilled with daily prayer and an hour of worship on Sunday. If we make God our first priority, nothing else in our lives will be left unchanged. Our abiding love for

God will affect how we deal with the people we meet, how we understand our jobs, where we spend our time and our money, which relationships we pursue.

Once we decide what our priorities are, we need to make sure we put our resources there. Any number of corporations and political administrations have floundered because they forgot this critical step. Clearly stated priorities, an inspiring mission statement, and an elegant strategic plan can never succeed if they fail to move from words to actions. Setting new priorities without changing entrenched processes and structures is a recipe for failure. A company's assertion that customer satisfaction is its top priority rings hollow when calls go unanswered for lack of staff or when shoddy products are not improved. Political leaders are called out for hypocrisy when they promise a new day and proceed with business as usual.

If we want to pursue different priorities, we have to get out of the trap of business as usual. There is a common saying, attributed to Albert Einstein, that insanity is doing the same thing, but expecting different results. Sometimes it seems as though we live in a time of mass insanity. We say we want our lives to be different, but we don't change what we do. We want to lose weight but do not stop eating fast food every night. We want to save more money but we keep buying everything we want. Continuing to do the same thing will not result in the changes we want. Similarly, it is futile to realign your priorities if you are not willing to change the way you act. The same road will lead to the same destination. If you seek a new destination, you need to follow a new path.

Putting God First

If you want your relationship with God to be your top priority, you need to find the path that draws you closer to him. But, of course, you can't figure out where you need to go unless you know where you are. So, the first step to moving forward is finding out where you are.

Taking an inventory of your faith life is a good first step:

- How often do you pray?
- Have your forms of prayer changed over the years?
- Do you pray alone or with others?
- Do you go to Mass regularly?
- Do you take your faith values into consideration when making moral decisions?
- When deciding how to spend your time or money?
- Do you read spiritual books? Listen to the Catholic programming available on television, radio, or online? How often?
- How often do you participate in classes or other opportunities to learn more about your faith?
- Do you seek spiritual counsel from reliable guides?
- Do you seek to form your conscience well or just do what feels good at the moment?
- Do you discuss your faith with others?
- Do the people who know you know that you are a person of faith?
- Do you look at the world, especially other people, with eyes of faith?

The purpose of the inventory isn't to make you feel guilty. After all, if you inventoried your pantry before grocery shopping, you wouldn't feel guilty that you were out of flour. Instead, you'd know what was missing, what you need to seek out. In the same way, this inventory will help you know where you need to shore up your faith life and where you need to devote more time and effort.

Of course, that means you have to find that time and energy. The easiest way to free up those resources is to eliminate waste. No matter how organized and focused we are, we all waste time and energy on things that do not reflect our stated priorities. Lurking throughout our busy days are traps that lie in wait to steal our precious time and energy.

One of the most common traps is the trap of "urgent but not important." The ease and immediacy of digital communication has made this trap even more prevalent. We find ourselves giving priority to answering the text message or e-mail or phone call, not because it's important, but because we've accepted the premise that immediate communication requires an immediate response. Constant interruptions from the various gadgets in our lives keep us from sustained attention to our conversations and tasks and even prayer. How many of those interruptions really require our immediate attention? How many reflect our real priorities?

Procrastination is another favorite trap. We can always find a reason to delay doing the things we know we need to do. "I'll go back to Mass once Lent starts." "I'll volunteer at the soup kitchen once I finish my big project at work." "I'll start praying the rosary—beginning in May." "I'll join the parish Bible study once my work travel lessens." "I'll go to confession before Christmas." "I'll pray just as soon as I fold the laundry and load the dishwasher. Oh yeah, and iron something to wear to work." Sound familiar? There's always something else to be done—and there always will be. Making excuses steals your time and energy. By the time you've explained to yourself why you really don't have time to pray today, you could have prayed a psalm, offered up an intercession for a friend who is struggling, or just sat quietly repeating Jesus's name.

I'm a runner. I hate running, but I love having run, so I had to make a rule. Once I've made three excuses as to why I can't run, I have to run. If I have a good reason not to run (perhaps there's a lightning storm or I have a fever), I don't keep making excuses to convince myself. Next time you start making multiple excuses, stop, take a deep breath, and admit that you don't have a good reason to procrastinate.

A more insidious trap is the one that says no effort is worthwhile unless it's total. You don't want to do it unless you can give it one hundred percent! Falling into this trap, people trying to strengthen their spiritual lives undertake a life of spiritual discipline that would intimidate a cloistered nun, all while trying to work full-time, in the home or outside, and be a loving family member. It's the spiritual equivalent of starting an exercise program by running a marathon. At first, it's invigorating, but all too soon the struggle begins (not to mention the cramping), making it easy to just abandon the effort all together, deciding that it's a waste of time and energy or that it's just beyond your capacity. Setting realistic goals and striving for growth over time is far more likely to succeed.

A common trap in our culture is the need to be productive *all the time*. The benefits of spiritual development, of making God your priority, are frequently internal and subtle, easily missed by the casual observer. A person who lives in an intimate daily relationship with God will be more patient, more willing to help, and will have a more peaceful and joy-filled spirit. But, as Ebenezer Scrooge would say, "None of these puts a penny in a man's pocket!" In a culture that measures value by productivity, these benefits are easily dismissed. In a perverse twist of perception, the things of most lasting value are seen as having little worth.

A much more difficult way to free up time and energy is to eliminate activities or practices that do not reflect your priorities. These activities might be good things, but they must give way to more important things. Only you can decide if a regular meeting with a spiritual director is more important than serving on another committee for the home-school association. Finding a balance that reflects your true priorities (God, family, friends, service, rest) is not easily accomplished. It will require delicate adjustments over time, but it's worth the effort.

Keeping a Priority Focus

What steps can you take to make putting God first a habit?

First, you need to give your relationship with God your best time. Spend time with God when you are at your best. If you are a morning person, try to start your day with some time for prayer and spiritual reading. If you are a night owl, block out some time before bed. Though God loves us even when we're at our worst, that shouldn't be all he gets.

Second, you need to treat your time with God as an appointment. Our calendars are filled with things we must do: meetings and conference calls, dental appointments and errands, ballet lessons and basketball games, dinner parties and deadlines. We'd hesitate to cancel these scheduled events. Why shouldn't we give our relationship with God the same consideration, putting "appointments" with God into our calendars?

Third, it's important to schedule "God time" first. It's way too easy to decide that God will get the time we have left. Of course, there's almost never any time left. Work expands to fill the time available. (I'm pretty sure that's a law of physics.) We'll struggle to find a few scraps of time to squeeze in prayer, or the parish faith formation class, or some spiritual reading. Set aside time for God *before* you start adding the extras.

Fourth, time with God needs to be part of your daily life. Strengthening your spiritual life isn't something that happens apart from the rest of your life, in carefully isolated periods (though dedicated periods for prayer are important). You can listen to a Catholic radio program while you make dinner. You can pray a decade of the rosary with your kids while you drive to soccer practice. You can read a spiritual book while you wait in the doctor's office or ride the subway. These practices have the added benefit of giving witness to your faith in the public square. But this doesn't work in reverse. The homily at Mass is *not* the time to catch up on e-mail.

Finally, you need to think twice before making new commitments of time or energy. You can't do everything. (Those people you see on television who seem to do it all? They have behind-the-scenes staff making it all possible!) If your life is already full and you decide to take on a new commitment, you have to let something go. The best way to choose is to examine each commitment in light of your priorities. What truly matters to you? Following the first commandment means that your relationship with God is your top priority. Everything else you do must be viewed through the prism of that relationship. If God is first, all is well.

Points to Remember

- Our priorities deserve the conscious commitment of our resources. The first commandment reminds us that God must be our ultimate priority.
- Strengthening our spiritual lives requires intentional effort over time. We must take care to avoid the traps that would steal our energy and distract us from our ultimate goals.

Culture Connection

In the film *Up in the Air*, main character Ryan Bingham gives seminars in which he encourages those attending to imagine themselves free of the burdens of possessions, commitments, expectations, and relationships. He encourages them to travel through life with the minimum of carry-on baggage. The only thing he seems to value is building up his frequent-flyer account. Through a series of personal encounters throughout the film, he comes to question the priorities around which he has structured his life. Like Ryan, each of us has had encounters and experiences that forced us to rethink our priorities and reclaim our values. Where do we want to go?

Role Model: Cardinal Joseph Bernardin

Cardinal Joseph Bernardin served as archbishop of Cincinnati for ten years and as archbishop of Chicago for more than fourteen years, until his death from cancer in 1996. Despite his hectic schedule shepherding some of the largest dioceses in the United States, Cardinal Bernardin was noted for beginning every day in the same way: with an hour of prayer in front of the Blessed Sacrament. His staff was carefully instructed not to interrupt him for any reason—even a phone call from the pope!

Cardinal Bernardin's priority was clear: God came first. Always. In the last years of his life, he became a model of forgiveness and of pastoral care for the seriously ill. In the weeks before his death, he wrote to the U.S. Supreme Court, asking them to show respect for the dignity of those near death. Despite his suffering, his priority never wavered. He loved God most of all. Because of that priority, he loved God's people, especially those in greatest need.

Try This

For a week, spend a few minutes before bed thinking through your day and answering the following questions, writing your answers in a journal:

- What task or relationship got most of your energy today?
- Did your efforts reflect your true priorities?
- What one step can you take tomorrow to help ensure that your priorities and your efforts align?

Each morning, upon waking, read your response to the final question. Make a special effort to take whatever steps are needed to ensure that you are expending your efforts well.

Talk It Through

- How have my priorities changed in the last year? The last five years? Has this change been positive or negative?
- How have I organized my life to reflect my priorities?

Pray

Lord,

I love you.

Without you, my life has no anchor

and I drift from day to day.

Help me to keep my love for you at the center of my life

so that I may steer a steady course.

Amen.

CHAPTER TWO

THE SECOND COMMANDMENT
Seeking Intimacy

You shall not take the name of the LORD,
your God, in vain.

At first glance, the second commandment seems almost quaint. The notion of refraining from using God's name casually outside of the context of prayer may seem odd when OMG is such a common phrase that even the text-illiterate know what it means.

Traditionally, this commandment has been understood as a warning to guard our language, to avoid speaking about God and holy things casually or with disrespect, and to refrain from swearing to false oaths by God's name. The civility of public discourse would certainly improve if we took more care in our speech, eliminating coarseness and casual uses of God's name. At the same time, a greater love and respect for sacred things would allow us to delve more deeply into the mystery of God.

But, if we look more closely at this commandment, we can see that it makes even greater demands on us. The second commandment calls us to develop the habit of intimacy with the God who made us. To understand the demands of this commandment, let's take a look back.

From the Burning Bush to the Word Made Flesh

In one of the most striking scenes of the Old Testament, God calls to Moses from a burning bush, charging him to be the one who would lead the people of Israel from slavery in Egypt into the Promised Land. Stunned by the vision and the call, and acutely aware of his own limitations, Moses asked why the people of Israel would ever believe that he was God's prophet. In response, God tells Moses his name. While this may seem casual, it is actually an act fraught with meaning. As the *Catechism of the Catholic Church* explains, "God confides his name to those who believe in him; he reveals himself to them in his personal mystery. The gift of a name belongs to the order of trust and intimacy" (*CCC,* 2143).

This notion may seem odd to us. Today, telling someone your given name is casual, even meaningless. You know the first name of the person who waits on you at a restaurant and who answers your panicked call to the computer help line. Even new acquaintances greet you by your first name. But this informal affability is a rather new development. As late as the mid–twentieth century, it was considered impolite to address someone by his or her given name without permission. In earlier times, knowing and being invited to use someone's given name was the mark of an intimate relationship, limited to family and extremely close friends.

God's decision to share his personal name with Moses and the people of Israel was an invitation to intimacy. It was also an act of trust. God trusted that they would not treat his revelation lightly and take his name in vain. Much of the Old Testament is the story of God's relationship with the people he had chosen to be his own. The people he had invited into an intimate, eternal relationship. The people to whom he had confided his name.

Intimacy with God requires mutual respect and self-revelation. That doesn't mean that it stifles the heartfelt expression of honest emotion, even if that emotion is negative. One need only look at the book of Psalms to realize that the people of Israel didn't hesitate to share their joy, fear, pain, and even anger with God. Still, reverence for God underlies every word in the Psalms.

God's self-revelation reached its climax in the incarnation of Jesus. In the incarnation, God himself became human and chose to live among us. Through baptism, we become the adopted sons and daughters of God, members of the body of Christ. It is no accident that we are baptized by name since, by baptism, we are drawn into that intimate relationship with God.

Living in Intimacy With God

In popular speech, an "intimate relationship" is often a thinly veiled euphemism for a sexual relationship. However, not all intimate relationships are sexual and not all sexual relationships are intimate.

A truly intimate relationship is marked by self-revelation and self-giving love. In Jesus Christ, God has given us the perfect model of the love at the foundation of an intimate relationship. Jesus reveals God through his words and actions. He poured out his love throughout his ministry, culminating in the ultimate gift of self on the cross. After the resurrection, when he returned to his Father, he sent his Holy Spirit to his followers to be with us always, to teach and to guide, to continue fostering the relationship between Christ and his body, the Church. Still today, the Spirit continues to work in and through the Church.

So how can we seek the intimacy with God to which our baptism—and the second commandment—calls us? What habits do we need to develop so that we continue to grow in our relationship with the God who loves us?

Before all else, we must believe that God does love us. We are made in the image and likeness of God and, as such, we have intrinsic worth. We don't need to earn God's love. He grants it freely and unconditionally, a pure gift of grace. We can share our truest self with God—the good and the bad, the strengths and the weaknesses, the hopes and the fear—all the while recognizing that God loves precisely that truest self. We need hold nothing back.

That kind of honesty takes practice. Developing the habit of sharing our true selves with God will take humility and trust. We are used to working hard to make a good impression at an interview, on a first date, in front of family and friends. We try to save face instead of admitting our failures. We shift blame instead of taking responsibility. Sharing our true selves with God means that we humbly admit our flaws and failures, trusting that God's love for us will not waver.

We must replace the bad habits that encourage us to hide our true selves and pretend to be what we are not with three habits that will draw us closer to God and will help us find the intimate relationship with him for which our hearts long.

The first habit we need to foster is the *habit of prayer.* Our human relationships teach us that no relationship can survive, let alone thrive, without honest communication. Prayer is, quite simply, communication with God. We speak to him and he speaks to us. Thus, communication requires both talking and listening. In prayer, we lay before God all the aspects of our lives, good and bad. We offer him the praise and adoration he deserves simply because he is God. We must also listen for God's response, often through the words of Scripture or simply in the silence.

As a rule, prayer does not happen by accident. (Prayer before pop quizzes in math or while in search of a parking space is excepted.) We need to be intentional about setting aside time to pray. If our only time for communicating with God is the occasional Sunday Mass, we are selling the relationship short. What intimate relationship can survive with an hour a week (or less!) of communication? If you spend more time talking to your Facebook friends than to God, things may be out of balance (and you've answered the question of where you'll find the time to pray. The computer has an off button for a reason.).

No matter how busy you are, you can make time to pray several times a day:

- Before leaving the house each day, say a brief prayer of thanks for a new day and for the grace of having a job (if you are so fortunate). This doesn't need to take longer than it takes you to lock the door.
- Before you start the car, say a prayer asking God to accompany you on your journey. (And a prayer for patience probably wouldn't go awry!)

- Grace before meals gives us a chance to express our gratitude to God and to recall the needs of those who lack the basic necessities of life.

- If you have a spouse or children, praying together is a wonderful way to bring the family together and to model an intimate relationship with God for the children. Children are strongly affected by watching their parents. Why not give them a good example, helping them develop habits that will lead them to God?

- A more extended period of daily prayer should be the norm. The time for this prayer depends on your schedule. It should be at a time when you at your best and unlikely to be interrupted (turning off the cell phone will help). You may want to set aside a place in your home suitable for prayer. Keeping a Bible, a crucifix, and your journal there will facilitate your prayer. If your kids interrupt you (for non-emergencies), invite them to join the prayer.

Getting into the habit of prayer teaches us to call on God's name, not in vain, but trusting that he will hear and answer us.

The second habit that will help to deepen our relationship with God is the *habit of reconciliation*. We begin by opening our hearts in honesty and examining our actions, identifying when we have and have not been faithful to the God who loves us. We admit our faults, express honest sorrow for our betrayal of this most important relationship, and commit to changing our way of living as we move forward. In the Catholic Church, these steps are ritualized in the sacrament of reconciliation. Reconciliation celebrates God's love and forgiveness. These gifts wait for those who ask for them. Through the action of the priest,

God absolves our sins and we begin anew. A regular celebration of this sacrament will foster the intimate relationship we desire with God.

On a daily basis, our prayer time might include a brief examination of conscience, looking honestly at the times we failed to live in accord with God's commandments, to live in self-giving love. Such reflection should lead us to an expression of sorrow for our failures and stir in us the desire for the sacramental celebration of God's forgiveness.

Finally, to draw closer to God in the intimate relationship to which he calls us in the second commandment, we must learn the *habit of awareness.* We can hear a text message arrive from across the room, but we don't notice the presence of God. God is present in our lives and in our world if only we take time to notice. By cultivating the habit of awareness, we notice the hand of God in the beauty of nature and in the loving people who surround us, in the moments that bring us joy and in the comfort that heals our sorrow. By being aware of God's presence in our lives, we are moved to sing praise to God's name, an act that is never in vain.

Points to Remember

- By revealing his name to Moses, God invited the people of Israel into a relationship with him. The Old Testament is the story of that relationship. God's relationship with the human race reached its culmination in Jesus, God made flesh.

- In baptism, each of us is called into an intimate relationship with God, becoming his adopted sons and daughters and members of the body of Christ. That relationship is the heart of the Christian life.

- This intimate relationship with God requires that we share our true selves, trusting that God loves us as we are.
- To find the intimacy we seek, we must develop the habits of prayer, reconciliation, and awareness.

Culture Connection

In the film *Lars and the Real Girl*, a socially awkward young man named Lars, unable to form bonds with the people in his town, introduces a life-size doll as his fiancée, Bianca. Rallying behind him, the people accept Bianca into the community, treating her as if she were, in fact, a real girl. Over the course of time, through their loving acceptance of Lars as he is, the people of the town give him the strength and security he needs to begin reaching out to the people around him, forming the new bonds of intimacy and care that he needs. Step by step, Lars learns how to develop the close and loving relationships on which the human community depends.

Role Model: Moses

You can't really talk about the Ten Commandments without talking about Moses. Moses led the children of Israel out of slavery in Egypt, through forty years of wandering in the desert, to the entrance into the Promised Land (though Moses did not enter the Promised Land himself). God gave the Ten Commandments to Moses on Mount Sinai, setting the foundation for the covenant between God and his people.

Moses had a uniquely intimate relationship with God. It was to Moses that God appeared in the burning bush, confiding his name. In addition, Moses was the first prophet, called to speak to the people on God's behalf. But he was unique among all the prophets—he saw God face to face. No other prophet saw God. Now, Moses's relationship with God was not always smooth. Moses often questioned God, expressing his doubt and even anger. Through it all, the intimacy of their relationship never wavered until the day of Moses's death. The final words of the book of Deuteronomy give his epitaph:

> Since then no prophet has arisen in Israel like Moses, whom the LORD knew face to face, in all the signs and wonders the LORD sent him to perform in the land of Egypt against Pharaoh and all his servants and against all his land, and all the great might and the awesome power that Moses displayed in the sight of all Israel. (34:10–12)

Try This

For a week, spend a few minutes before bed thinking through your day and answering the following questions, writing your answers in a journal:

- How did I encounter God today?
- How did I respond when I met God in the events of my day?
- What parts of myself do I share when I encounter God? What do I hold back?

At the end of the week, see if you have become more attentive to the opportunities you have to encounter God. Does greater attention alter the way you respond to these opportunities?

Talk It Through

- What steps can I take to get to know God better?
- How can I share more of myself with God and with others?
- How do I show my love and reverence for God?

Pray

Loving God,

you have promised to be with me always,

strengthening me in your love and compassion.

Help me to always share my true self with you,

confessing my sins and asking you for all I need.

May I place my trust in you,

knowing that your love is faithful.

Amen.

CHAPTER THREE

THE THIRD COMMANDMENT
Spending Time

Remember to keep holy the LORD's day.

Well into the twentieth century, following the third commandment by keeping the Lord's day holy was a societal norm. The day began with a family trip to church, everyone well-groomed and dressed in their "Sunday best." After church, families returned home for Sunday dinner, typically the most lavish meal of the week, attended by extended family and friends. Virtually all businesses were closed, often in accord with local laws, so it was a day for leisure and relaxation shared with those closest to us. People saved their best—clothes, food, time—for God.

Over the last fifty years, the societal practice of keeping the Lord's day has slowly eroded. The laws requiring that non-emergency businesses close on Sunday were restricted or repealed, meaning more people had to work. Youth sports leagues scheduled full slates of games, interrupting family time. Attending church services stopped being the centerpiece of the day. People started choosing the Mass they would attend based on what else was scheduled for the day, not infrequently attending Mass dressed in the clothes they would wear for their later activities, whether it was soccer practice or power-washing the porch. Sunday dinner became a thing of the past (outside of food commercials and lifestyle magazines). Sunday has become just another day—a last chance to run errands before a new work week begins.

The pace of life never seems to abate with no day of rest. Should we care about this change? How does it affect the relationship with God that we are trying to foster?

Let's Start at the Very Beginning

Though keeping the Lord's day holy is the third commandment, it has its roots in the Bible's very first pages. The book of Genesis tells us that, having labored for six days over the work of creation, God rested on the seventh day.

Scripture scholars often contrast the account in Genesis 1—2 with a Babylonian creation myth which arose in the Ancient Near East, not far from the land of Israel. According to the Babylonian creation myth, the gods created human beings not out of love or a desire for union, but because they wanted servants. In the Babylonian view, we humans have value only as long as we serve the gods. When we cease being productive, our value fades away.

In contrast to this depressing view of humanity, the book of Genesis tells us that, as human beings are made in the image and likeness of God, we are called to follow his example with regular rest from our labors. God's command that we keep his day holy is a powerful testament to our intrinsic dignity and our value to God. Through our labor, we share in God's work of creation, but God does not love us only because we are productive. Our value to God derives not from what we do but from who we are—precious creations, children of God, born with dignity.

The prophets, particularly Amos, tied observance of the Sabbath to respect for other people, especially the poor. To him, those who chafed at the requirement to keep the Lord's Day holy were likely to do unholy things on the other six days of the week as well:

"When will the new moon be over," you ask
"that we may sell our grain.
And the sabbath,
that we may open the grain-bins?
We will diminish the ephah,
add to the shekel,
and fix our scales for cheating!
We will buy the destitute for silver,
and the poor for a pair of sandals,
even the worthless grain we will sell!" (Amos 8:5–6)

It may seem that the Sabbath gets a bit of bad press in the New Testament. Not infrequently, Jesus is at odds with the authorities because he heals on the Sabbath. The religious leaders, following the letter of the law, point out that Jesus has six other days on which he can heal. Jesus responds by affirming the dignity of those he heals, noting that there is no need to leave them to suffer for even one more day, once again tying the Lord's Day to an affirmation of human dignity. After Jesus's death and resurrection, the early Christians began to celebrate the day of the resurrection, Sunday, as the Lord's day, a practice that most Christians continue today. This shift is most appropriate. Nothing affirms the intrinsic value of human beings as does the death and resurrection of Jesus. God was willing to die that we might live with him forever.

A Question of Time

The first three commandments highlight the three interrelated qualities that are essential to any successful relationship: priority, intimacy, and time. Time may be our most precious resource. It is certainly the only resource which is strictly limited. No matter how hard we try, we cannot make more time. What we can do is learn how to spend it well, in accord with our priorities and in ways that allow us to share our true selves.

Unfortunately, our contemporary understanding of time is surrounded by myths. The most common myth is that our various gadgets will buy us more time. Certainly, some inventions have proved to be huge time-savers. Using a washing machine requires far less time than pounding clothes against a rock beside a stream or boiling large pots of water and scrubbing clothes against a washboard. Similarly, cooking is far simpler and less time-consuming when it does not require gathering wood and tending a fire. The lives of women in many developing nations are changed dramatically when their village gets a well, eliminating long walks to get fresh water.

But many gadgets, though they have definite time-saving aspects, actually turn out to be time-wasters. For example, while a cell phone with Internet access makes getting driving directions far easier, it also tempts us to waste time surfing the Net. Making it a habit to harness the value of our gadgets without falling into the trap of wasting time is essential to keeping the focus on our relationships.

One of the most destructive myths is the myth of "quality time." According to this myth, it doesn't matter how *much* time we spend with those we care about; only the *quality* of that time matters. This myth gives priority to planning special events and downplays the importance of everyday interactions. But it is in the habit of those daily interactions with those we love that the relationship is strengthened. No trips to the theme park or special date nights will ever replace more mundane activities like sharing chores and meals, going for walks, or simply conversing as ways to deepen a relationship.

The obvious corollary is that the habit of daily prayer and at least weekly participation in the Eucharistic liturgy will do more to strengthen our relationship with God than periodic attendance at Mass on major feast days or rare but intense periods of prayer while on retreat or in times of great need. We are far less likely to share our true selves at occasional "special events" than in the daily interactions that form the fabric of our lives.

The Habit of Spending Time With God

Deciding how we spend our time is one of the most important moral decisions we make in the course of a day. What controls your schedule? What determines which activities fill your days? What time does God get in your daily schedule? It is all too easy to drift from day to day, filling our hours with errands, tasks, and events, with no plan that highlights our priorities. At the end of a day, a week, or a year, we note that time has slipped away but we can't say how we spent it.

If that description sounds familiar, what are your options for change? First, you can change the way you plan your schedule. A new way of planning your schedule requires that you understand time as a resource and have a clear sense of your priorities. Think of your schedule as a budget for your time. In planning a budget, you set aside money for savings, to pay your mortgage, to buy groceries, to make your car payment, and the like. The bills that are most important get paid first with any leftover funds being available for discretionary use. Budgeting your expenses based on what seems most convenient at the moment is a sure recipe for financial trouble as you pay for dinners out but miss car payments.

Applying the budgeting example to your daily schedule means that your first step is to set aside time for your priorities. If your relationship with God is a priority, that means setting aside time for daily prayer, spiritual reading, regular participation in the Eucharistic liturgy, and regular reception of the sacrament of reconciliation. Then, it's time to add in family time, work responsibilities, community service, and relaxation.

Now, the difficulty with this plan comes when allotting time for all these things means either no sleep or the need for more than twenty-four hours a day. The former is unhealthy in the long term and the latter is impossible—at least in the short term. I suppose we can hope someone will invent time travel, allowing us to buy more time, but I don't think we should count on that.

Another option is to carve out a small amount of time on a regular basis. Rather than trying to find large blocks of time, look for five minutes. Can you set aside five minutes each day, perhaps time spent waiting for a meeting to start or for football practice or karate class to end? Do you spend five minutes on mindless channel surfing? Or five minutes playing computer solitaire? If you identify five daily wasted minutes each month, at the end of the year you'll have found an extra hour each day. You can use that hour (or the increments as they accrue throughout the year) to build your relationship with God, by reading the Bible, saying the rosary, or stopping in the church for a brief visit to the Blessed Sacrament. It's amazing how those minutes accumulate and how much you can do with them.

You might also decide to commit to keeping the Lord's Day at least once a month for a period of time (three months, six months, a year). Begin the day by attending Mass and then spend the rest of the day in leisure (shopping, movies, or other activities that require that other people work to entertain you don't count) or volunteering at a local food bank, homeless shelter, or the like. Prepare a meal and eat together (it's not rest if one person has to do all the cooking and cleaning up!) Go for a walk, read, pray the rosary together, play a game, visit with family or friends. If at all possible, make the day electronics-free. That means no computer, television, texting, or video games. Enjoy a day of rest and see if it makes a difference in your week.

As discussed earlier, it often seems impossible to find time for everything. In some cases, the time crunch may be temporary, even if it lasts for several weeks or even months. Dealing with a newborn, the illness of a spouse or a parent, or a particularly challenging project at work could make a schedule especially tight. In such cases, knowing your priorities is even more important. If times of great stress become times when you let go of the things you truly value, you will find yourself adrift and heading for the rocks, like a ship without its anchor. In times of great stress, only your top priorities can have your time. Keeping the Lord's Day holy and putting God's time first will help you stay on course.

Points to Remember
- Keeping the Lord's Day has deep biblical roots in both the Old and New Testaments. These roots are based on our need to follow God's example by resting from our work.
- Keeping the Lord's Day is an affirmation of our intrinsic worth as children of God.
- Scheduling time to spend with God in prayer and worship is key to maintaining the intimate relationship with God that is our first priority.

Culture Connection
Watching *The Devil Wears Prada*, it's easy to get distracted by all the fabulous clothes and beautiful people. But then you'd miss an important element of the story. All of the characters employed at *Runway* magazine have sacrificed their lives and relationships to the magazine's glossy pages. Not even the seemingly all-powerful Miranda Priestly can keep her relationships intact when she gives top priority and the overwhelming majority of her time to her job. They all want to believe that, in the end, the sacrifice will be worth it, but might they be relying on a false hope? "What profit would there be for one to gain the whole world and forfeit his life?" (Matthew 16:26).

Role Model: Nelson Mandela

Today, Nelson Mandela is best known as a Nobel laureate and as South Africa's first president elected after apartheid fell and people of all races were allowed to vote. But before these achievements, he was a prisoner for twenty-seven years, most of them spent in an island prison off South Africa's coast.

Twenty-seven years in prison can change your perspective on time. In his time in prison, Nelson Mandela learned the value of patience and using his time well. He learned to listen and pursue compromise. He learned to seek truth and offer reconciliation. His efforts, though imperfect, helped to bring healing to a nation wounded by decades of pain and injustice.

Try This

For a week, spend a few minutes before bed thinking through your day and answering the following questions, writing your answers in a journal:

- On what tasks did I spend my time today?
- Did I waste time performing unnecessary tasks or engaged in meaningless entertainment?
- Did I foster both my need for productivity and my need for relaxation?

At the end of the week, see if you can identify patterns in how you spend your time. Are you most productive at certain times of the day? What distractions pull you away from what you want to be doing? How can you use this information to make sure that the relationships of greatest value to you get your best energy?

Talk It Through

- How do I keep the Lord's Day holy? How do I want to spend my Sundays?
- What determines how I spend my time?
- Does my appointment calendar reflect my values?

Pray

God of all ages,

my time on earth is limited, help me to use it well

balancing work and rest,

all in praise of you

so that, in time, I may live with you forever.

Amen.

CHAPTER FOUR

THE FOURTH COMMANDMENT
Giving Respect

Honor your father and your mother.

With the fourth commandment, the focus changes from our relationship with God to our relationship with our brothers and sisters. These relationships are closely related. As the First Letter of John states clearly, "If anyone says, 'I love God,' but hates his brother, he is a liar; for whoever does not love a brother whom he has seen cannot love God whom he has not seen" (1 John 4:20). Our protestations of love for God ring hollow if they are not accompanied by kindness, compassion, and generosity toward those around us.

When he gave the two great commandments, Jesus called his followers to love their neighbors as they love themselves. This commandment assumes a healthy self-love. This sort of self-love is not narcissism or arrogance. It develops from the first three commandments, out of the recognition that each of us is a precious child of God, made in his image and likeness. True self-love is founded in the intrinsic dignity that provides a sense of security and peace which, in turn, allows us to love others wholeheartedly.

Five of the last seven commandments deal with our relationship with others, beginning with one of the most intimate of all human relationships, that of parent and child. Over time, the commandment has been understood more expansively to include all relationships of authority. As the *Catechism of the Catholic Church* explains:

> The fourth commandment is addressed expressly to children in their relationship to their father and mother, because this relationship is the most universal. It likewise concerns the ties of kinship between members of the extended family. It requires honor, affection, and gratitude toward elders and ancestors. Finally, it extends to the duties of pupils to teachers, employees to employers, subordinates to leaders, citizens to their country, and to those who administer or govern it.
>
> This commandment includes and presupposes the duties of parents, instructors, teachers, leaders, magistrates, those who govern, all who exercise authority over others or over a community of persons. (*CCC*, 2199)

Authority in a Cynical World

In the last century, the notion of authority has eroded in all aspects of life, fostered by the dislocations caused by political and economic events including the Great Depression, two world wars, and the decline of colonialism. In the latter half of the twentieth century in the United States, the Vietnam War and the aftermath of the Watergate break-in caused a radical decline of faith in political institutions. At the same time, many people lost faith in social institutions as social orders based on divisions of race, class, and gender began to crumble.

The Catholic Church was not immune from these waves of change. In the wake of the Second Vatican Council, the Mass underwent its most significant change in almost five hundred years. Even the most casual observer would notice the changes in structure and the shift from Latin to the language of the people. At the same time, religious orders reformed, with many moving away from their traditional dress and entering more fully into the world around them. Dissent on a variety of topics, most famously artificial birth control, became more prominent. Increasingly, even people who self-identified as religious became far less likely to accept the Church as a source of authoritative teaching.

More recently, this general decline in the acceptance of authority has continued. With the rise of democracy around the world, people expect a greater say in their rule and their destiny. In many minds, authority has become equated with authoritarianism, forcing people to accept beliefs not their own. People respond to leaders with cynicism, doubting that authority is wielded on behalf of the common good. In our digitally connected world, people turn to crowd-sourcing and user forums to share and learn, rather than seeking answers from authorities. They seek out blogs and other media that reinforce their views, accepting as reliable only those who agree with them.

The notion of authority has changed in the business world as well. A variety of business experts railed against top-down methods of leadership, encouraging business owners to give workers more authority to solve problems, improve processes, and implement suggestions. In later developments, the compensation of top executives became disconnected from the success of the companies they led. Compensation no longer was the reward for leading people well.

Families experienced the same shifts, though on a more intimate scale. African American families migrated from the Deep South to the growing urban industrial centers of the North. Other families moved from tightly knit ethnic enclaves into the rapidly expanding suburbs. Multigenerational families living in close proximity grew increasingly less common as the twentieth century drew to a close. The greater availability of divorce, particularly the rise of no-fault divorce, made family bonds ever more fragile. Blended families with often unclear lines of authority grew more numerous. As the twenty-first century began, sociologists and religious leaders were beginning to discuss a marriage crisis as the age for marriage steadily increased and more couples cohabited without benefit of marriage.

In a world with such seemingly fragile bonds of family and authority, what does it mean to honor your father and mother?

Authority and Respect

In grade school religion classes, catechesis on the fourth commandment typically focuses on the importance of obeying your parents and teachers and, generally, being respectful to all adults. This focus is certainly helpful for young people in their formative years. Parents are children's first and best teachers. As children grow up, their parents (or those charged with raising them) must help them learn how to make good choices, based on lasting values. Through their actions, even more than their words, parents model right relationships with God, self, others, and things.

A wise teacher once told me that the primary job of parents and teachers is to make themselves redundant. As adults, we shouldn't have to call our fifth grade math teacher when we need to balance our checkbooks or rely on our mom and dad to tell us to eat our peas, write a thank-you to Aunt Beatrice, and go to Mass on Sunday. If our parents and teachers have done their jobs well—and we have learned our lessons well—we are equipped to leave home and parental authority and set off to develop independent lives and healthy relationships.

Do these natural life changes render the fourth commandment meaningless? If not, what does it mean for our lives once we are no longer dependent on our parents for care and guidance?

Clearly, the fourth commandment doesn't disappear from our lives when we hit eighteen (or twenty-one or fifty) or even once our parents die. This commandment reminds us that there will always be someone with authority over us. To follow the fourth commandment well, we must develop the habit of respect. The habit of giving respect to those in authority, while maintaining a healthy self-respect, is the foundation for stable and harmonious interpersonal relationships.

But what is respect (apart from a classic Aretha Franklin hit)? Respecting people in authority means recognizing the weight of responsibility they carry because of their positions, acknowledging the skills and experiences that led them to this position, trusting them to use those skills and experience to make good decisions, and following their direction. It requires humility. We need to accept that we don't always have the answers—or the information we need to get the answers. We don't necessarily see the whole picture, so we must defer to those who lead.

The habit of respect means giving your best to assist those in authority in their efforts. For example, an employee shows respect to his boss by doing the tasks assigned to the best of his ability, by providing all relevant information to aid in decision-making, and by working toward the stated goals with commitment and energy. A citizen shows respect to political authorities by staying informed about the political process, voting, attending community meetings, paying taxes, and following just laws.

Now, respecting authority is not the same thing as blind obedience. People in authority can and do make mistakes. As we grow older, we are better able to see the flaws in our parents, teachers, and other leaders. In fact, in our teenage years, it seems that's all we can see! We are under no obligation to obey those who would lead us astray or who ask us to do something that violates our consciences. True respect means accepting the other's flaws and limitations.

While recognizing the good that those in authority do, we must make judgments about when to follow and how to dissent. Obviously, emergency situations where people are endangered or laws are broken are exceptional situations. Even when expressing our disagreement, we need to show respect and honor the authority of the individual. One way to do this is by stating our values clearly, without anger or condescension. Identifying the conflict with our values shows respect for the person in authority and for ourselves. Another way to dissent respectfully is to offer alternatives without denigrating the original idea, recognizing that our alternatives may not be adopted and accepting that defeat with good grace.

The March of Time

As we noted above, the way we live the fourth commandment changes over time. The way a nine-year-old honors her parents is far different from the way a forty-nine-year-old does. As we mature, we honor and respect our parents by incorporating the values they taught us into our lives, using these values to make wise choices and to contribute to the world around us. As our parents grow older, our situations may be reversed. Rather than receiving our parents' care and attention, we may find ourselves in situations where we must care for our parents and ensure that their needs are met. In those cases, honoring our parents requires sacrifice and patience. We may have to sacrifice our time to run additional errands or to make visits, our money to provide financial and physical security, and even some privacy if we need to share living space.

Even when our parents continue to live independently, sacrifices and patience may be needed. Calls to check in, hearing the same news again and again, listening to the same stories of the "good old days" can tax our patience. They don't feel productive. They don't move our life plans forward. They don't seem to accomplish much of anything at all. But these gifts of time are the building blocks of relationship and the foundation of honoring those who raised us. To honor is to give of oneself in gratitude.

The Flip Side

Most discussion of the fourth commandment looks at our obligations to authority. But does this commandment say anything to us when we are the ones who have authority? Should it guide our actions when we are the ones in charge?

The fourth commandment makes it clear that the default option is to respect people in positions of authority. We don't withhold respect from our parents, waiting to see if they measure up. Soldiers join an army with the expectation that they will respect their commanding officers. But even if respect comes with a position, it can be lost. Those in authority cannot act without care and concern for their charges. A parent who leaves small children alone at home while out partying with friends will lose their children's respect and may, in fact, lose custody of the children. A military leader who recklessly places soldiers in harm's way may be relieved of command.

Surprisingly, exercising authority requires humility, just as respecting authority does. No leader will ever succeed who is certain that he alone has all the answers. Believing that you and only you can ensure the success of the enterprise is the key ingredient in the recipe for disaster. On the other hand, recognizing and admitting to your limitations and seeking any necessary assistance is the hallmark of effective leadership. A leader who welcomes new ideas and inputs, calling forth the best in those over whom she has authority, is a leader that others will want to follow.

Exercising authority is a challenging task. Truly great leaders keep an open mind when others express disagreement. Authority isn't about having all the answers. It requires attention to the needs of others, a firm commitment to clearly stated values, and the willingness to make difficult decisions and accept responsibility for their consequences. The best leaders (and, make no mistake, parents are leaders) spend much of their time listening, identifying the needs and values of those around them, and learning from the experiences of others. Asking questions, weighing options, and, when necessary, admitting mistakes are the hallmarks of leadership that inspires respect.

Points to Remember

- The fourth commandment addresses our relationship with those who have authority over us. In the last century, traditional notions of authority have eroded and have often been replaced with cynicism.
- Respect is our proper response to those in authority. Respect does not mean blind obedience, but it recognizes the responsibility that leaders carry and tries to assist as much as possible.
- The way we honor our parents changes through the course of our lives, but it always requires patience and sacrifice.
- The fourth commandment makes demands on those who are in authority as well. When we find ourselves in positions of authority, we must take care of those in our charge, making decisions for the common good.

Culture Connection

The family has been a staple of the situation comedy since the earliest days of television. (Actually, it goes back to radio, but I don't!) From *Ozzie and Harriet* to *Father Knows Best*; from *The Waltons* to *The Brady Bunch*; from *The Cosby Show* to *Roseanne*; from *Everybody Hates Chris* to *The Middle* television sitcoms have depicted families in all their variations, with all their joys and angst.

Now, life is rarely as simple as depicted in some television sitcoms. Unfortunately, most of life's problems aren't resolved in thirty minutes (with time for commercial breaks!) nor are parents either as all-knowing or as bumbling as they are all too often depicted. But at their best, these sitcoms portray the underlying realities of family life: children learning to respect the wisdom, experience, and authority of their parents and parents helping their children grow into the best people they can be.

Role Model: Eunice and Sargent Shriver

Eunice and Sargent Shriver were the brains and energy behind two organizations that had their roots in profound respect for others, particularly those easily disregarded. Sargent Shriver was the founding director of the Peace Corps, a U.S. Government agency that sends people (old and young) to foreign countries to live and work with the people there. The volunteers (who, though not paid for their service, do receive a modest living stipend) assist with development and educational projects. Even more important, they live as friends and neighbors, treating those they serve as persons worthy of respect, recognizing the dignity that comes from shared humanity.

Eunice founded the Special Olympics, literally in her own backyard! This organization allows children and adults with developmental disabilities to compete in a variety of athletic contests. The underlying value of this organization is respect: for the potential of the competitors; for the gifts they bring to the activities; for the value of the time and friendships shared between those with disabilities and those without. The Special Olympics' message of respect has spread beyond the athletic field to classrooms, community groups, and everywhere people of good will gather.

Try This

For a week, spend a few minutes before bed thinking through your day and answering the following questions, writing your answers in a journal:

- What was my relationship with the people I encountered today?
- How did I treat those under my authority? Did I listen to their ideas and concerns? Did I make decisions for the common good?
- How did I interact with those in authority over me? Did I give my best? How did I show respect? Express my disagreement?

At the end of the week, review your encounters, looking for patterns. Where do you need to show greater sacrifice and patience? Where do you need to speak up more?

Talk It Through

- How do I handle responsibility?
- How can I be a better child? A better sibling? A better parent? A better boss?
- How do I show respect for those who have authority over me?

Pray

God,

we ask you to bless those in leadership positions.

Give them wise and discerning hearts

and a spirit of selflessness,

so that they will lead well.

Imbue us with a spirit of respect and humility

so that we may always follow in your path.

Amen.

CHAPTER FIVE

The Fifth Commandment
Recognizing Dignity

You shall not kill.

"I have set before you life and death, the blessing and the curse. Choose life, then, that you and your descendants may live, by loving the LORD, our God, obeying his voice, and holding fast to him" (Deuteronomy 30:19–20).

With these words, Moses presents a stark choice to the children of Israel: They can choose the path God has set out by means of the commandments or they can follow their own path. One path leads to life and blessing and to God, their ultimate source. The other path leads to death and destruction, away from God who is the author of all good things. As might be expected, our choice of path determines our destination.

The fifth commandment summarizes this choice of path: You shall not kill. Choose life, not death. But what does that mean?

Matters of Life and Death

On the surface, this seems to be the easiest commandment to follow. After all, homicide statistics indicate that a relatively small proportion of the populace will ever kill another human being. If you think you may be part of that number, I strongly recommend that you stop reading here and seek professional help.

If you've decided to keep reading, you must begin by recognizing that this commandment is not a free pass. It does not mean: Avoid committing homicide and all is well. Truly abiding by this commandment requires a much greater effort. It requires recognizing the intrinsic dignity of each and every human being, formed in the image and likeness of God. "Every human life, from the moment of conception until death, is sacred because the human person has been willed for its own sake in the image and likeness of the living and holy God" (CCC, 2319).

Significant cultural forces may make it difficult to respect human dignity. Increasingly graphic movies, television shows, and video games have desensitized us to violence. Because of the prevalence of such violent images in these media, the real consequences of violence often fail to engender the horror they should. On the other hand, scientific developments have made it increasingly easy to see human beings as commodities, to be designed according to exacting specifications. Already, newspapers discuss the possibility of "farming" body parts to extend life or conceiving children genetically designed to meet specific aesthetic standards of hair and eye color and body type or to be organ donors for other family members. Such efforts are hardly affirming of human dignity since they treat human beings as products rather than individuals with intrinsic value.

Of course, the Church teaches that the fifth commandment forbids any action that intentionally ends the life of an innocent person. These forbidden actions include not only murder, but euthanasia, assisted suicide, and abortion as well. It is worth noting that Church teaching does recognize that lives may be taken in self-defense. If someone is attempting to harm you, you may resist, even to the point of the attacker's death. On the other hand, we are under no obligation to take every possible step to preserve life. Thus, a person with a very serious illness may choose to forgo extraordinary treatments if such treatments are too burdensome and unlikely to be of significant benefit.

Taking all reasonable efforts to preserve life is another part of following the fifth commandment. Reckless behavior, including speeding and aggressive driving and driving under the influence, violates this commandment because it puts life at risk for no good reason. Though addictions have an involuntary element because substances create a physical and emotional dependence, we do choose to take the first puff or the first drink or the first pill. And we choose whether or not to seek help.

Simply put, we should never hold in our hands the power over the life and death of any human being, including ourselves. Only God can create life; only God can decide when it ends. We do not get to decide whose life is worth living. The value of a life is based not on its present or future productivity. Each human being is imbued with value from the very first moment. Formed in the image and likeness of God, each human being has an intrinsic dignity and value.

Beyond Life and Death

The need to recognize this intrinsic dignity makes following the fifth commandment a challenge. Anything that destroys or detracts from another person's dignity violates the commandment. Of course, sins against this commandment vary in degrees of seriousness. Calling someone a name is not as grave as killing someone. But, really, as you develop in your spiritual life, is your standard of judgment really going to be: It's not as bad as if I killed someone?

The belief that the fifth commandment goes beyond actually taking another's life goes back to Jesus who extended this commandment to include anger and even insulting language: "You have heard that it was said to your ancestors. 'You shall not kill; and whoever kills will be liable to judgment.' But I say to you, whoever is angry with his brother will be liable to judgment, and whoever says to his brother, 'Raqa,' will be answerable to the Sanhedrin, and whoever says, 'You fool,' will be liable to fiery Gehenna" (Matthew 5:21–22).

Prejudice can kill hope and possibility, diminishing the lives of those we dismiss without knowing them, viewing them as stereotypes rather than individuals. Generations of human beings saw their human development curtailed because of their race, sex, disability, nationality, or religion. Amazingly, prejudice, accompanied by bias and discrimination, still exists. Language that categorizes groups of people as less than human makes it easier to rob people of their human dignity. In the movie *Hotel Rwanda*, which chronicled the genocidal violence in that country, the perpetrators of the violence commonly called their opponents "cockroaches." Diminishing their humanity made it far easier to kill them. In less dramatic ways, prejudging groups of people makes it easier to ignore them and the claims they may make on us, robbing them of their dignity.

The power that words have to harm is all too evident. News reports are filled with tragic stories of hate crimes where taunts and insults give way to violence. In recent years, we have seen an appalling rise in bullying, especially among young people. Individuals and cliques isolate young people who seem to be different, killing their spirits and diminishing their dignity by calling them names, ridiculing them, and sharing private information. Digital communication makes it easier for these insults and revelations to spread broadly, increasing the pain and the shame. In some tragic cases, the despair caused by intense bullying has led to the suicides of the victims, literally taking their lives. Even in the less extreme cases, the wounds to the dignity of the victims are grave and long-lasting.

Finally, we must recognize that our daily decisions may affect the ability of others to live in dignity. We make political and economic choices that have broad impact. We can vote with our wallets, choosing a candidate based on what his or her policies will mean for our standard of living rather than considering how these policies will promote the common good and protect the most vulnerable members of society. We can buy the cheapest items available, regardless of what that means to the laborers who create them. It's certainly easier than seeking out those companies that pay fair wages and provide safe work environments. Making purchases and investment decisions with a view to their broader impact requires time and effort.

Being Life-Giving

This chapter would come to an abrupt end if I just said, "Don't kill anyone and avoid violence unless you're being attacked." It would also be far less useful in aiding your spiritual development. So let's look more deeply at the habits you need to follow the fifth commandment.

The habit of recognizing the dignity of each human being is the habit of being life-giving and thinking of others first, measuring our words and actions by their intent and their impact. We need to develop the habit of considering the broader impacts of even our seemingly mundane choices. This is not a habit easily or swiftly acquired.

A serious evaluation of our political and consumer choices is a long-term effort requiring substantial research. On the political side, it is not sufficient to read a candidate's speeches, full of flowery language and promises. A candidate's past actions are an important consideration in any decision. We must also remain attentive to political leaders between elections, holding them accountable for their decisions and expressing our concerns for those who are most vulnerable—the powerless and voiceless.

Similarly, in making consumer choices, it is helpful to look at a firm's labor practices (both here and abroad), its oversight of its suppliers, and its involvement in the community. Does the firm respect the dignity of its workers, customers, and shareholders or is profit its only concern? Fortunately, the Internet makes such information far more accessible, though reading this information requires a critical eye and a commitment to regular monitoring.

We can also develop our ability to recognize the dignity of all persons by our choice of volunteer activities and community service. Obviously, we will choose activities that carry a personal meaning. For example, we may volunteer at the school that educates our children or help to raise funds for a disease that afflicts a favorite aunt. We can choose based on the business contacts the activity will provide or on its comfort and convenience. However, at least some of our service should focus on those whose dignity is most endangered: those who are poor, unborn, homeless, ill, disabled, elderly, immigrant, or imprisoned. Putting ourselves into situations where we come into direct contact with the vulnerable teaches us to recognize the God-given dignity that each person possesses. Jesus taught us that, in caring for these most vulnerable ones, we actually care for him (see Matthew 25:31–46). The more time we spend in service to the least among our brothers and sisters, the easier it will be to see in them the face of Christ.

Recognizing the dignity of other persons requires that we control our anger and sarcasm, a great challenge for many people. It is far too easy to lash out in anger, especially in times of particular stress. We can get laughs by making a cutting joke at another person's expense. The old practice of taking a deep breath, counting to ten, and saying a Hail Mary may sound old-fashioned, but it works. Its purpose is to buy time to make us think about what we are doing, to allow us to act rather than react. The minute spent breathing, counting, and praying is enough time to reconsider speaking in anger. It buys us time to frame our words more carefully and with greater charity.

On a daily basis, we must strive to remove prejudice and stereotype from our language. It's easy to scoff at such a recommendation as "political correctness," but that dismissal discounts the power of words. The childhood rhyme, "Sticks and stones may break my bones, but words will never harm me" is simply wrong. Words may not leave visible fractures and lacerations, but their ability to wound and to leave deep, though unseen, scars cannot be denied. If our words imply that people have no value, it is all too easy to reflect that view in our actions. Ignoring the needs of the poor and vulnerable, or blaming them for their difficulties, may allow us to live with greater comfort, but it does nothing to enhance the dignity which is God's gift to every human person.

Points to Remember

- The fifth commandment calls us to respect the dignity of every human person. As such, it forbids any action that intentionally takes the life of an innocent person, including homicide, euthanasia, abortion, and assisted suicide. The fifth commandment also requires that we avoid those actions that heedlessly risk our own lives or the lives of others.

- Words and actions that damage or destroy the dignity of other people violate this commandment as well. These sins include lashing out in unjust anger, prejudice, and bullying.

- Developing the habit of recognizing the God-given dignity of each person requires consistent effort over a period of time. Researching the impact of our choices, controlling our anger, measuring our words, and caring for the most vulnerable will make it easier to recognize the dignity with which God has gifted each person.

Culture Connection

It's certainly easy to find films and video games filled with violations of the fifth commandment. In some games, players score points based on the players' speed and effectiveness in killing "the enemy." In film and television, improved special effects have made the graphic depiction of violence and mayhem ever more common. But let's look at some examples that offer a more complex rumination on human dignity.

The *Hunger Games* trilogy, a series of books targeted to the teen market, gives a horrifying view of what happens when human dignity is ignored and people are treated as instruments to be used by those in power. In the *Hunger Games*, twenty-four young people are forced to fight each other to the death for the amusement of the highly privileged ruling class. The knowledge that their children can be condemned for others' entertainment adds to the burden of the people, the vast majority of whom labor in degrading conditions and constant fear and deprivation to ensure that the elite continue to live in comfort. The heroine of the trilogy, Katniss Everdeen, struggles to determine what human dignity means in a world where she and everyone close to her are treated as tools in the hands of the powerful.

A very different view of human dignity appears in the lyrics of Lady Gaga's hit song, "Born This Way." Written to offer support to victims of bullying, the song repeatedly affirms that we do not have to earn the right to dignity. Nothing we do or do not do, nothing that we are or that we become, can take away our dignity. God has gifted all people with dignity. Quite simply, we are "Born This Way."

Role Model: Rose Hawthorne Lathrop

Rose Hawthorne was the daughter of Nathaniel Hawthorne. (Yes, that Nathaniel Hawthorne—the one who wrote *The Scarlet Letter*.) She was received into the Catholic Church as an adult. After she was widowed, she became a great advocate for the terminally ill, promoting what we now call palliative care and hospice care. She even founded an order of religious women to provide this care, among the first groups to focus on caring for the terminally ill. Under the religious name Mother Alphonsa, she founded houses where those approaching death could receive care that respected their dignity as precious children of God.

Try This

For a week, spend a few minutes before bed thinking through your day and answering the following questions, writing your answers in a journal:

- What were the three most important choices I made today?
- What impact did those choices have on the dignity of others?
- What role, if any, did that impact have on my decision?

At the end of the week, review the choices you have made. As you went through the week, did you become more aware of the impact of your decisions? If so, how did that affect your decision-making process?

Talk It Through

- What individuals or groups do I find it easiest to perceive as less than human? What steps can I take immediately to begin changing that perception?

- What practices do I find most successful in helping me guard my temper and my tongue?
- What can I do in my world to help promote the dignity of those who are most vulnerable?

Pray

God,

you are the author of all life.

You craft each human being

in your image and likeness.

You endow each person with a dignity

that can never be lost.

Let us see the face of your Son in all human beings,

especially those who are most vulnerable.

Help us to recognize and affirm the dignity of all.

Amen.

CHAPTER SIX

The Sixth Commandment
Maintaining Integrity

You shall not commit adultery.

It's likely that more ink has been spilled on this commandment than on any other. Love, sex, marriage, and betrayal are constant themes in art, literature, and film—not to mention in the supermarket tabloids. Though each generation seems to believe that they have invented sex and scandal, it's been around from the beginning. (If you don't believe me, give Genesis a read. You'll get all the sex and scandal you want— rape, incest, near-adultery, and prostitution—as well as couples that truly love each other.)

Of course, past generations didn't have access to two things that have had a significant effect on modern sexual relationships: effective contraception and the Internet. Though birth control in some form has existed for millennia, its effectiveness and ease of use improved dramatically in the late twentieth century. For the first time, contraception allowed people to reliably separate sexual activity from the possibility of childbearing, lessening the consequences of extramarital sexual relations. Sexual content is pervasive on the Internet. Because it is accessed privately and anonymously, the Internet has created uncountable sites offering pornography, cybersex, and ease of access to casual sexual relationships. It often seems as though discretion, modesty, and shame are forgotten concepts.

Possibly due to these modern developments, it may seem as if our culture is divided into two camps: one that seems to hold that all sins are sexual and another that seems to hold that nothing sexual is a sin as long as the participants are of age and give consent. Neither of these views accurately reflects the demands the sixth commandment places on us.

The sixth commandment is about more than sexual fidelity in marriage. The Church has always understood this commandment to prohibit any sexual activity outside the bonds of marriage. Furthermore, it prohibits those activities within marriage that do not express the full meaning of both sex and the marriage relationship. At its heart, the sixth commandment is about living with holistic integrity, so that words and actions make the same promises.

Promises, Promises

Marriage is founded on the exchange of promises. In the Latin Church, the core element of the sacrament of marriage is the exchange of vows between the couple. The priest or deacon witnesses the vows and blesses the couple, but they marry each other. That exchange of promises is the key—not the rings or the dress or any of the other elements that make planning a wedding an expense and a chore. In their vows, a couple promises each other an indissoluble, exclusive relationship that will endure through the natural ups and downs of life. They agree to enter into an intimate sharing of all aspects of their lives, placing the common good of the marriage and the family that may result ahead of their self-interest.

Because of its indissolubility and exclusivity, a marriage is a sure foundation for building a family, giving security to the children brought into the family by birth or adoption. A healthy, loving marital relationship creates a stable environment where children can develop and grow.

The marriage promises create a safe place for the spouses' self-revelation and total self-gift. The sexual relationship of a married couple literally embodies the promises at the foundation of the marriage. A sexual relationship must be exclusive and indissoluble, a complete gift of self, one to the other. Adultery violates the promises of marriage by taking away the exclusivity. Various forms of "trial marriages" take away the permanence. Any other activity which takes away from the total self-gift in a marriage, as contraception does, also violates this commandment.

On the other hand, the sixth commandment prohibits sexual activity in relationships that are not marriage. Such relationships lack the indissolubility and exclusivity that are necessary for a complete gift of self. Without the commitment that the marriage promises provide, most people hold back a part of themselves, not giving completely.

Even more grave are those sexual interactions in which one person is used as an object to gratify the desires of the other, with little to no regard for the needs, feelings, and dignity of the partner. Prostitution, rape, and pornography are among these serious offenses.

A Question of Integrity

When we use our bodies to promise relationships that do not exist or to damage existing relationships, we are not living with integrity. *Integrity* derives from the word meaning "whole." Thus, a lack of personal integrity means that the relationship between body, mind, and soul has become disrupted so that we cannot share all of ourselves with those we love. Living with integrity allows us to build our relationships on solid ground.

But what does living with this integrity mean in practice? Is simply refraining from extramarital sexual relationships sufficient?

Avoiding evil is always the first element of following the commandments. However, not engaging in activities that violate the sixth commandment is only the beginning. We must strive to strengthen our relationships. To understand how to strengthen a marital relationship, it is helpful to look back to the qualities that relate to the first five commandments. The word *integrity* is also closely related to the word *integrate*. It makes sense that we would need to bring together—to integrate—the qualities we develop by following the other commandments.

In the first commandment, we focused on priority. A healthy marriage is the priority human relationship for both partners. Resources, most especially time and energy, are committed to helping the marriage remain strong and to deepening it as time passes. In a sacramental marriage, the spouses place great priority on their relationship with God, with shared and individual prayer, including attending Mass together. Shared prayer can also help a family strengthen the bonds that unite it. Even simple practices such a grace before meals, lighting an Advent wreath, and blessing family members at key life moments can aid a family in its efforts to grow closer to God and to each other.

The second commandment encourages us to seek intimacy. Clearly, any healthy marriage is an intimate relationship, a relationship in which both spouses feel safe enough to reveal their true selves. In marriage, this intimacy exists at all levels as the spouses share their bodies and their emotions, as well as the concerns of daily life.

This intimate sharing requires the commitment of time, as we discussed in our look at the third commandment. Couples that do not spend time together will find it very difficult to maintain the loving intimacy of the relationship. Couples forced to live apart due to military deployment or other unavoidable circumstances must take special care to tend the relationship while apart. In such cases, digital technologies that allow video chats and other forms of contact are extremely useful. Lack of time spent together is a major factor cited by couples analyzing their marital problems. Given the fast pace of modern life, a shared effort is needed to commit to spending time together. Both spouses must be willing to let go of other activities to make time to spend together in prayer, conversation, shared activities, and sex.

Respect underlies the fourth commandment and is, likewise, an essential element of the marital relationship. A marriage in which the partners do not respect each other is destined for grave difficulties. Spouses must respect one another's gifts, needs, and contributions to the marriage. Over the course of a marriage, those contributions may vary and the partners may trade off the "heavy lifting" of the relationship. Throughout the marriage, each partner will contribute in his or her own way. Failure to respect your spouse's contributions shows a lack of gratitude. Failure to contribute can make him or her feel taken for granted. Neither situation is conducive to the loving self-gift at the heart of marriage.

Finally, in our discussion of the fifth commandment, we looked at the intrinsic dignity of each human person. No marriage can survive if one partner fails to recognize the dignity of the other. Unfortunately, we cannot ignore the fact that this is the case in many relationships. Failure to recognize the dignity of a spouse is characteristic of marriages marked by serial adultery or abuse (verbal or physical). Even if the problems in a marriage do not rise to the level of abuse, not recognizing a spouse as a partner with equal dignity is destructive. Among those who are not married, failure to recognize the dignity of other persons or of oneself may reveal itself in promiscuity, either using others as instruments of your own pleasure or allowing yourself to be used in such a way.

To make living with integrity a habit requires that we unite all of our efforts to follow the commandments and apply them to our most intimate relationships. By reflecting in our bodies what we believe in our hearts and put into action in our lives, we follow the sixth commandment.

Points to Remember
- The sixth commandment prohibits sexual activity outside marriage and those activities within marriage that do not express the full meaning of both sex and the marriage relationship.
- The promises of indissolubility and exclusivity create a safe place for the spouses' self-revelation and total self-gift. The sexual relationship of a married couple embodies these promises.

- When we use our bodies to promise relationships that do not exist or to damage relationships that already exist, we are not living with integrity.

- To live with integrity, we must bring together all we have learned about following the commandments.

Culture Connection

If it weren't for this commandment, country music might have nothing to sing about. Some of the greatest songs of country music have addressed the issue of extramarital affairs from every possible angle. Hank Williams's classic *Your Cheatin' Heart* speaks of the impact on the one committing adultery and the consequences of self-deception. Dolly Parton's haunting *Jolene* tells of the anguish suffered by the spouse who is betrayed while Carrie Underwood's *Before He Cheats* lauds the revenge she seeks. In each of these songs, the failure to keep the promises made causes pain and disrupts relationships. It leaves everyone involved feeling diminished in some way.

Other country songs approach the issue of relationships more positively, trying to maintain integrity. In Jason Aldean and Kelly Clarkson's duet "Don't You Wanna Stay," the partners struggle to move beyond the temptation of temporary pleasure to find something more lasting and true to the depth of their feelings for each other. Perhaps the most poignant country music tribute to the integrity that underlies any healthy, long-lasting intimate relationship is Keith Urban's "Making Memories of Us." It's no wonder he chose to sing it to his bride on their wedding day!

Role Models: Tobiah and Sarah

The book of Tobit introduces one of the most unusual love stories in the Bible. Tobiah is traveling to his father's hometown to pick up some money deposited there. When he gets to Media, he meets his kinsman Raguel who has a daughter named Sarah. Sarah has been married seven(!) times, but none of her husbands has survived the wedding night. Despite this rather frightening history, Tobiah falls in love with Sarah at first sight and marries her. On their wedding night, Tobiah and Sarah pray this prayer :

> Blessed are you, O God of our ancestors;
>
> blessed be your name forever and ever!
>
> Let the heavens and all your creation bless you forever.
>
> You made Adam, and you made his wife Eve
>
> to be his helper and support;
>
> and from these two the human race has come.
>
> You said, "It is not good for the man to be alone;
>
> let us make him a helper like himself."
>
> Now, not with lust,
>
> but with fidelity I take this kinswoman as my wife.
>
> Send down your mercy on me and on her,
>
> and grant that we may grow old together.
>
> Bless us with children. (Tobit 8:5–7)

(Spoiler Alert: Tobiah does more than survive the night. He and Sarah become the parents of seven sons!)

Try This

For a week, spend a few minutes before bed thinking through your day and answering the following questions, writing your answers in a journal:

- What did I do today to strengthen my most important relationship?
- Did my actions reflect the reality of this relationship?
- Was I divided in how I shared my love with those closest to me? If so, how?

At the end of the week, reflect on how much time and effort you put into your most intimate human relationship. Are you living the promises that underlie this relationship? If not, where are the gaps? How can you fill them?

Talk It Through

- What cultural attitudes promote the division of sex from relationship? What steps can I take to heal that division in my own life?
- What activities and attitudes are most important to strengthening intimate relationships?
- In what ways do I live the promises I have made?

Pray

Lord,

you created human beings male and female

and invited them to share in your own creative power.

Help us to respect the power of this gift

and to use it with care and integrity.

May we love truly, whole-heartedly, and selflessly.

Amen.

CHAPTER SEVEN

THE SEVENTH COMMANDMENT
Living Gratitude

You shall not steal.

With the seventh commandment, our attention turns to our relationship with things. In many ways, following this commandment may be the toughest challenge for many people today .

Turn on the television and you can channel surf from a shopping channel to an infomercial showing you products that "will change your life"—for just $29.95. And call *right now* and get free shipping. Use the special promotional code and we'll double your order! Then you can go online and buy still more stuff, comparing products and prices to make sure you get the best deal. Of course, a few weeks later, you can go back to the television to check out a "reality" show that will help you deal with the clutter or manage your money better so you can afford everything you want. If you decide to leave your house, you can drive past strip malls and big box stores—and self-storage facilities—on the way to the mall. When clutter management and storage solutions are a growth market, it's easy to see that our relationship with things has grown out of control.

Innovation is the order of the day. No matter what we buy, there's always something newer, faster, and better just around the corner. Some days, it seems you've barely pulled out of the store parking lot before your purchases have become obsolete. Some stores even offer a guarantee that they'll buy back your purchase (at a reduced price, of course) if you upgrade the item within a specified period of time. The market strategy seems to assume that you'll be buying something new soon. Buying more and getting less seems to be the watchword of the culture.

It is said that St. Francis of Assisi opposed allowing his friars to own books, but not because he didn't want them to read or to gain knowledge. Rather, if a friar owned a book, it was only a matter of time until he'd want a shelf to put it on, and so it would go from there, to the detriment of the Franciscan commitment to poverty in solidarity with the vulnerable members of society.

Experience has shown that Francis was right. Possessions seem to carry within themselves the seeds for their own multiplication. I buy a new television which means I really need to get more channels and the accompanying digital video recorder since I can't possibly watch everything. And since the picture is so much better, I should probably get a new video gaming system. And then, of course, I'll need a bigger and better media center to hold it all. In the same way, the purchase of a new dress means new shoes, some earrings, a purse, and a cute scarf. The desire to own more feeds on itself and becomes as bloated as our closets and storage bins.

The Dangers of Accumulation

Despite the variety of television shows depicting people who are physically overwhelmed by their possessions, slowly being buried alive beneath a leaning tower of discarded magazines and DVDs is not the greatest danger we face from the excessive accumulation that runs rampant in our society. Instead, we should fear allowing our key relationships to be put out of balance by a burgeoning desire to get more and to make sure we keep what we have. The desires to accumulate and possess are not the foundation of the healthy relationship with things to which the seventh commandment calls us.

First, an unbalanced relationship with things can damage our relationship with God. Focusing our energy on accumulating, organizing, renovating, and playing with our stuff leaves little room for God to be our priority relationship. Working to earn more money, managing that money, and purchasing and maintaining what that money buys leaves little room for quiet time and prayer and for keeping the Lord's Day holy. We risk allowing wealth and possessions to become the strange god we place ahead of the Lord.

An unbalanced relationship with things can also damage a healthy and appropriate love of self. It is easy to begin measuring your worth by what you have rather than by the sort of person you are. Owning the right things takes priority over doing the right things. Such a view allows too much of our self-worth to depend on external factors, such as the opinions of others. Our value comes from the fact that we are created in the image and likeness of God. Whether we are millionaires or beggars, we are of equal value in God's sight.

Finally, a relationship with things that is out of balance can be damaging to our relationship with others. We might begin believing that we have earned what we have and that our possessions are a just reward for the efforts we have made. This feeling may reflect an appropriate pride in one's work. However, the danger is that it might engender the view that the poor deserve their poverty. After all, if possessions are the reward for effort, it stands to reason that lack of effort explains the lack of possessions.

This attitude is expressed in many ways, most commonly through complaints that the poor are lazy and unwilling to work. At one time, many people believed that worldly success was indicative of God's approval. In such a worldview, poverty showed God's disfavor, making efforts to alleviate poverty unnecessary as they would go against God's will. Subscribing to this view absolves us from caring for those in need. A modern variant of this view is the so-called "prosperity gospel." According to this philosophy, God wants everyone to enjoy an abundance of worldly goods. Failure to enjoy prosperity is easily viewed as resulting from a personal lack of faith.

None of these attitudes accurately reflect the teaching of Jesus as related in the Gospels. Throughout his earthly ministry, Jesus showed a clear partiality for those who were poor, proclaiming that they were blessed by God. Though it led to criticism from the leading citizens of his day, Jesus spent his time with sinners and outcasts. He encouraged his followers to give up their possessions and follow him. Jesus seems to have been poor himself, lacking a permanent place to live and being supported throughout his ministry by contributions from some of his followers. He died owning nothing. His executioners divided his last few possessions. Even his tomb was borrowed. Jesus was not a man who equated things with success. Why would an abundance of possessions be an indication of his favor?

From Grasping to Grateful

Living this commandment and following Jesus's example requires that we begin to treat our possessions as gift, receiving them with gratitude. We must understand ourselves as stewards rather than owners.

So what's a steward? Generally, a steward is responsible for caring for property that he doesn't own. For example, a person with several homes might hire a steward for each home. The stewards would live in or near the homes to ensure that they are properly maintained for the owner's use. To act as stewards, we must begin by recognizing that all things come from God. We use them and care for them, all the while awaiting the Lord's return.

A first step in learning to live as a steward is fasting. Fasting is one of the oldest spiritual practices. In the Old and New Testaments, people fast as a sign of their repentance or to prepare for some spiritual task. Fasting detaches us from our possessions, reminding us that God is all we need. Fasting also unites us more closely to the poor. As we go without voluntarily, we get a glimpse of what life is like for those who do not have basic necessities.

The traditional way to fast is to go without food (or with minimal food) for a specified period of time, usually a day. However, we can fast from things other than food. People fast from electronics, from entertainments, and from bad habits. To enhance the fast, you may wish to donate the money you would have spent to some appropriate charitable cause or to use the extra time you gain in prayer or volunteering to assist others.

While fasting is especially appropriate to the season of Lent, you may wish to choose one day each month as a day of fast. Periodic fasting will help you develop the habit of gratitude and keep your relationship with things on the right track.

In addition, several practices, if they become habits, can help us learn to live with the grateful heart of a steward:

- Say grace before you eat—even just a snack. A short prayer will remind you that even the basic necessities of life are gifts from God. These quick reminders throughout the day will help to keep your heart grateful.

- Be intentional about your purchases. The Internet has made purchasing extremely simple. A few clicks of a mouse and you can spend thousands of dollars without a second thought. And that's the point. All too often, these purchases happen without a second thought—or even a first thought. (Sorry, impulses aren't thoughts!) Such random accumulation of possessions whether or not a need exists is not the behavior of a steward.

- Don't acquire without giving. To reduce clutter, organizational experts often recommend the following strategy: Whenever you buy something new, you must get rid of something old. So, for example, you buy a new sweater, you must donate or discard an old sweater. Adopting this practice helps to stem the tide of acquisitiveness and helps to make sure you control your possessions rather than the other way around. In addition, your donated possessions may help to meet the needs of those who lack the necessities of life.

- Learn to savor. Don't mistake quantity for quality. Rather than truly enjoying our possessions, they are forgotten soon after acquisition. Pop quiz: Name five gifts you received last Christmas. How many of them did you really use and enjoy? How many are still in the box? Do you know where they are? A good steward will likely have fewer possessions but will fully enjoy each one.

- Don't limit thanksgiving to one Thursday in November (or one Monday in October for Canadian readers). Thanksgiving is the meaning of the Greek word that is the root of *Eucharist*. At its heart, the Eucharist is a celebration of thanksgiving for all that God has done and continues to do for us in Jesus Christ. Regular participation in the Eucharist reminds us that God is the giver of all good things and that our proper response is gratitude.

We must apply this concept of stewardship to our relationship with the earth as well. God commanded that human beings care for creation (see Genesis 1). When our desire for possessions overwhelms our care for creation, using resources without replacing them, we disregard God's command in favor of our own pleasure and comfort.

By striving to become good stewards, we will alter our relationship with things and find it easier to resist the myriad temptations to let things rule. When our relationship with things is in its proper place, we can give our relationships with other people greater attention. By living with greater simplicity and fewer possessions, we stand in solidarity with the poor whose lack of possessions is not a choice. As stewards, we own our possessions; they do not own us. Stewardship allows us to give more freely of our time, talent, and treasure to those in need.

Accepting our possessions with gratitude rather than as our just deserts helps us to be more aware of the human impact of our consumer choices. It changes how we understand what it means to get a "great deal." Instead of trying to buy more for less, we focus on buying things created fairly, respecting the people involved in their creation. We learn to treasure people rather than things. We show gratitude for everything we have, for the people who made it, and for the loving God who gives us all we need.

Points to Remember

- The seventh commandment addresses our relationship with things. This commandment calls us to move beyond accumulation and possession. We are not what we own.

- A burgeoning desire to get more and to make sure we keep what we have negatively affects our relationships with God, self, and others. This desire draws us away from the path Christ laid out in his life and ministry.

- To follow the seventh commandment, we must treat our possessions as gift, receiving them with gratitude. Seeing all we have as God's gift to us is the essential first step in living with a grateful heart.

Culture Connection

Few films more clearly depict the lure and dangers of unmitigated greed than *Wall Street*. For the main characters, Gordon Gekko and Bud Fox, nothing is more important than getting more—and no matter how much more they get, it's never enough. Rather than receiving their material goods with gratitude, they treat them as the spoils of war, won through their own hard work and thoroughly deserved. Nothing is more important than getting more wealth and the power that accompanies it, not even the people whose lives might be destroyed by their endeavors. But at the end of the day, what will remain?

Role Model: The Other Good Samaritan

As [Jesus] continued his journey to Jerusalem, he traveled through Samaria and Galilee. As he was entering a village, ten lepers met [him]. They stood at a distance from him and raised their voice, saying, "Jesus, Master! Have pity on us!" And when he saw them, he said, "Go show yourselves to the priests.'" As they were going they were cleansed. And one of them, realizing he had been healed, returned, glorifying God in a loud voice; and he fell at the feet of Jesus and thanked him. He was a Samaritan. Jesus said in reply, "Ten were cleansed, were they not? Where are the other nine? Has none but this foreigner returned to give thanks to God?" Then he said to him, "Stand up and go; your faith has saved you." (Luke 17:11–19)

I always think of this Scripture text as "the Thanksgiving Gospel" since it's typically read at Masses on Thanksgiving Day. Only one of the ten lepers who are cured returns to thank Jesus for the gift. Ten percent—great return on a savings account, not so good on a miracle. This miraculous cure transformed the lepers' lives. For fear of contagion, lepers lived with multiple restrictions which kept them separate from the community. Still, the Samaritan leper interrupts his journey to see the priests to return to Jesus. Cured lepers were required to show themselves to the priests in order to have all the restrictions lifted. So, the Samaritan stopped to say thank you before he enjoyed the benefit of the gift.

Try This

For a week, spend a few minutes before bed thinking through your day and answering the following questions, writing your answers in a journal:

- Did I buy anything today? If so, why did I buy it? Did I need it?
- How aware was I of the possessions I used today? Did I even notice them while I used them?
- What one thing was I most grateful for today?

At the end of the week, reflect on how often you make purchases or use possessions without thinking. Did the daily reflection raise your awareness? Did the reflection change your behavior?

Talk It Through

- What social forces disrupt my relationship with things?
- What effects do my possessions have on my relationships with God, myself, and others? Are these effects positive or negative?
- What steps can I take to become more grateful for the things I have?

Pray

Giver of all good gifts,
all that we have and all that we are
come from you.

Help us to receive things with a grateful heart
and, in gratitude, share what we have
with those who have little.
Amen.

CHAPTER EIGHT

The Eighth Commandment
Upholding Honesty

You shall not bear false witness against your neighbor.

"What is truth?" (John 18:38)

Pilate's question to Jesus continues to echo through the ages and lies at the heart of the eighth commandment. Unfortunately, throughout the ages, that question hasn't gotten any easier to answer. In fact, in some ways it's become more difficult.

In the digital age, truth seems to have become a crowd-sourced reality. The truth is whatever the majority of people say it is. Except not. Confusion seems to have grown between what is opinion and what is fact. Statements repeated endlessly and shared around the Internet are treated as fact, even in cases where the information they share is demonstrably false. More than a few reputations have been damaged by malicious gossip spread widely via social media.

The changing nature of the news cycle and the rise of tabloid and "citizen" journalism certainly haven't improved things. It's certainly good to get information about world events quickly. (Within an hour of the 2010 earthquake in Haiti, people around the world already knew about it and had started contributing funds for the relief.) On the negative side, the need to make information available quickly means less time to make certain that this information is accurate. In several instances, premature reports about the death of famous people have spread because of a single inaccurate report repeated across social media sites. Often rumor or speculation is presented as fact, only to require correction a few days later. Of course, there's no guarantee that anyone sees the correction.

Too many tabloid journalists make their livings by publishing rumor and speculation without concern for the effect on their subjects. Based on my extensive research, performed in grocery checkout lines and beauty salons, some celebrity couples seem to have been getting divorced (or married or pregnant) for at least ten years. These claims are typically supported by reports from "close friends." Though relatively few people treat these reports as anything other than the journalistic equivalent of fast food, providing momentary pleasure with no substance or value, being subject to such rumors must put a strain on any marriage or friendship.

Citizen journalists can provide an important service, reporting stories that would otherwise go unnoticed. They can also convey misinformation quite effectively. Several websites look surprisingly like news sites (and often have "news" in their names) but are actually places for individuals to post their own conjectures or promotional materials. In many cases, no one exercises any editorial control or provides any fact-checking. Other sites purport to be sharing news but are actually forums for like-minded people to exchange supposition and promote their views.

Given all these changes, it's not surprising that some people have even begun to doubt the existence of truth. Several years ago, a friend of mine and I were discussing our religious differences when he made a statement about something I believe. He said, "Well, that's true for you, but not for me." Taken aback, I objected: "It's either true or it isn't. It can't be both at the same time. I'll admit that I might be wrong (though I don't think so), but things can't be true and false at the same time. They just can't." Truth is no longer understood as an objective reality but as a consensus opinion or a personal conviction.

Honesty in a Digital Age

When truth is understood as a constructed reality, what does it mean to be honest? How do we tell the difference between welcome, and even necessary, honesty and indiscreet gossip? The *Catechism of the Catholic Church* summarizes this commandment as follows:

> The eighth commandment forbids misrepresenting the truth in our relations with others. This moral prescription flows from the vocation of the holy people to bear witness to their God who is the truth and wills the truth. Offenses against the truth express by word or deed a refusal to commit oneself to moral uprightness: they are fundamental infidelities to God and, in this sense, they undermine the foundations of the covenant. (*CCC*, 2464)

The eighth commandment requires that we uphold honesty, particularly with regard to our dealings with other people. Thus, it is an essential element of right relationships with others. At its most fundamental level, the eighth commandment requires that we tell the truth, but only the truth that needs to be told. Unnecessarily sharing secrets or information that would hurt another is prohibited as well. Rather than simply embracing the love of truth to which this commandment calls us, we tend to get hung up on specific cases of following this commandment, worrying unduly over whether it is acceptable to withhold a hurtful truth (it is) or whether it's acceptable to share a secret about someone being victimized or doing something harmful (it is). So, to summarize, it's fine to avoid the question, "Do these jeans make me look fat?" and to call the police if your childhood friend is being abused by her husband (or if she's the one doing the abusing).

What steps can we take to develop the habit of honesty? How can we live in truth in a world where even truth's existence is up for debate?

The obvious first step is to avoid lying. Not lying requires that we refrain from saying things that are untrue, from exaggerating the truth, from telling partial truths, and from acting hypocritically. Telling the truth can be much easier than lying. If nothing else, there's less to remember. You don't have to recall which lies you told to which people. Even though telling the truth may make life simpler, there will always be temptations to lie. We may want to avoid the consequences of the truth. We may want to avoid the shame or pain that telling the truth might bring. We may want to feel superior to those around us. We may want to hide our own failures or insecurities. We may desire to hold others to standards that we cannot meet.

Behind a life free of lies is a willingness to be truthful with yourself. Therefore, a right relationship with self is necessary. That right relationship starts with the belief that you are a beloved child of God, made in his image and likeness. That belief does not require that you ignore your faults and failures. In fact, an honest recognition of our faults helps us to recognize our need for the forgiveness that only God can give. But we must also realize that this forgiveness is readily available to all who seek it.

It is not enough to simply avoid lying. A second step in developing the habit of honesty is a willingness to attest to the truth. Like the characters in the children's story *The Emperor's New Clothes*, a surprising number of people are unwilling to say what they know or believe to be true. This is especially true when it comes to the question of faith. A willingness to speak up for your faith doesn't mean that you need to go door to door with a bag of tracts or to accost strangers on the subway to share the details of your spiritual journey. You can stand up for your faith by declining to engage in activity you believe is immoral or by grounding your arguments in the principles of your faith. You can gently call out behavior that offends. This doesn't require being rude or pushy. For example, you are at dinner with friends when one of them makes an inappropriate joke or a racist comment. All that is necessary is a statement like the following: "I'm sorry, but that language really bothers me. Please don't say things like that around me." No drama, no nastiness. Just a simple statement of what you believe.

A third step in developing the habit of honesty is discretion. Just because you strive to speak with honesty doesn't mean you have to say everything you know. Unfortunately, we live in an age of confessional reality shows on which people willingly share the intimate details of their lives in exchange for a few moments of fame. Social networking sites are filled with private revelations and photographs that should never see the light of day. The idea of keeping personal matters private seems outmoded and quaint to a culture where "too much information" is an unreachable standard.

As we discussed earlier, self-revelation is essential to the formation of intimate relationships. Discretion is the art of knowing what you should reveal and to whom. Just as failure to reveal your true self to those closest to you is damaging, so is sharing too much of yourself with those with whom you are more casually acquainted. Even more important is to hold in confidence the private information that others share with you (always presuming that keeping such information private does not risk their safety). Sharing private information is a betrayal that has a lasting impact on any relationship.

Full development of the habit of honesty requires a fourth step: speaking with charity. Some people equate honesty with uncharitable bluntness, but it is possible to be honest without being cruel. We need not share every thought and opinion. In cases where we must share a real concern, hurt, or offense, we can state our case simply, without anger, hurt, or condescension. Speaking with charity precludes engaging in hurtful gossip. Sharing information of another's failure or misfortune may lead to a fleeting feeling of superiority, but it is ultimately unsatisfying and damaging to existing relationships.

A final step in developing the habit of honesty is to learn to receive information with care. There's an old saying that if it sounds too good to be true, it probably is. We should be similarly careful about things that sound too bad. Rather than believing what we hear or read online or elsewhere, it's worth taking a few moments to research the truth before sharing. Being the person who stops the progress of a lie, even if only in your social group, is a valuable thing to be.

By following these steps, we can learn to uphold honesty and draw ever closer to the truth and to the God who is the source of all truth.

Points to Remember

- Truth is neither a constructed reality nor one choice among a series of equally valid options. Truth is an objective reality that accurately reflects what is. God is the source of all truth and love of truth leads us to greater love of God.

- The eighth commandment urges us to pursue the truth and to live in honesty, using our words with care.

- We must never fear giving voice to the truths of our faith, being willing to share what we believe.

- To keep this commandment, we must learn to avoid lies, speak with discretion and charity, and carefully assess the truth of information before we share it with others.

Culture Connection

Two highly lauded films show the two sides of honesty: the power of truth to heal and the power of a lie to destroy. In *On the Waterfront*, Terry, a dockworker and washed-up fighter, is called upon to testify against the dockyard mob boss, Johnny Friendly. Though he refuses at first, his girlfriend and a courageous priest ultimately convince him to speak the truth. Despite threats and great personal sacrifice, he perseveres. Though his honesty comes at quite a cost, it transforms the environment in which he lives, empowering others to stand together against evil.

In contrast, in *Atonement*, Briony's lie, born out of anger, misunderstanding, and jealousy, destroys the futures of her sister, Cecilia, and Cecilia's lover, Robbie. The effects of the lie spread through the film, poisoning relationships and cutting off hope. Once the lie has taken hold, honesty that comes too late cannot reverse the tragic consequences set in motion.

The power of truth. The power of a lie. Which will you unleash?

Role Model: Archbishop Oscar Romero

Though he served as archbishop of San Salvador for only a little more than three years, he stands as one of the Church's great speakers of truth in the twentieth century. He became archbishop during a time of political difficulty in El Salvador. (A military coup took place while he was archbishop.) During this period, the Church was persecuted; priests and nuns were murdered, tortured, imprisoned, and expelled from the country. The poor suffered greatly as all power rested in the hands of the wealthy and the military.

Archbishop Romero fearlessly spoke the truth, calling leaders to account and supporting the dignity and human rights of the poor. Not surprisingly, his truth-telling raised the hackles of those in power. They needed to shut him up. And so they did. On March 24, 1980,

Archbishop Romero was assassinated as he celebrated Mass. But his cause did not die and his voice rings out in all places where people speak of human rights and the dignity of all God's children.

Try This

For a week, spend a few minutes before bed thinking through your day and answering the following questions, writing your answers in a journal:

- Was I honest in my conversations today? If not, about what topics was I less than honest?
- Before I shared information with others, did I make sure that what I shared was true, charitable, and appropriate to share?
- Did I try to avoid receiving information that violated the privacy of others?

At the end of the week, look back over your entries and see if there is a pattern in the issues that challenge your attempts to be honest. Are there certain topics about which you are more likely to lie or to speak uncharitably? What steps can you take to change the way you address those topics or to avoid them all together?

Talk It Through

- What sources of information do I trust? Why do I trust them?
- How do I decide what sort of personal information I should share with people?
- In what circumstances am I tempted to lie? Why? Are there ways to avoid these situations or to change the way you act in them?

Pray

Jesus, you are the way and the truth and the life.

As we draw closer to truth,

we draw closer to you.

Help us to live our lives with honesty

and to guard our speech with charity,

that all we do may bear witness to your love.

Amen.

CHAPTER NINE

The Ninth Commandment
Promising Fidelity

You shall not covet your neighbor's wife.

Covet is one of those words that doesn't seem to exist outside the Bible. Really, when was the last time you heard someone use it in a non-biblical sentence? But just because the word has fallen out of use doesn't mean that the sins this commandment warns against have gone out of fashion. In some important ways, these sins have become even easier to commit.

Obviously, the ninth commandment is closely related to the sixth commandment, forbidding adultery. You might find it useful to think of coveting or desiring another person's spouse as a "gateway" sin. After all, you aren't likely to commit adultery with someone you've never desired. But breaching this commandment is a sin in its own right. Many more people are unfaithful emotionally than would ever dream of physical infidelity. Yet emotional affairs can be extremely damaging to the trust that underlies any healthy life-giving relationship.

As we discussed earlier, a sexual relationship, appropriate only in marriage, must be exclusive and indissoluble, a complete gift of self, one to the other. When one partner shares him or herself with a partner outside the marriage, the self-gift is compromised. You can't give all of yourself to two people. The math just doesn't work. Many married people consider emotional affairs to be an even greater betrayal of trust than a physical affair. An extramarital sexual relationship can be attributed to momentary bad judgment, alcohol, or unbridled lust. It is much harder to explain away an emotional affair since such affairs tend to be longer term and involve the sharing of thoughts, feelings, hopes, and fears. Even if an emotional affair never develops a physical dimension, the deep sharing in this extramarital relationship robs the spouse of what is appropriately reserved only to him or her.

Advances in communications have made it easier to carry on such affairs. Internet chat rooms facilitate anonymous conversations that invite unwise disclosures that can be the start of relationships. (There are even websites and chat rooms explicitly advertising their services for married people looking to meet new people. It should go without saying that "married dating" violates the ninth commandment.) Cell phones and text messaging make contact almost instantaneous. It was a bit more challenging to carry on an affair when keeping an assignation required the exchange of letters delivered by messengers on foot or by horse or when everyone in the community knew everyone else. Now, however, people can share words, sounds, and images across long distances in a matter of minutes. There's even a new word, *sexting*, for sharing sexually explicit images via picture mail. Frighteningly, the practice of sexting has been noted even among middle school students.

To be clear, the ninth commandment does not imply that all desire is wrong. The desire to be close to other human beings is natural and laudable. The desire for closeness and intimacy ties the human community together. Contrary to popular opinion, the Bible does not say that sexual desire is bad in and of itself. (If you doubt that claim, read the Song of Songs.) Desire to share yourself physically with your spouse is a good thing, drawing the two of you into an increasingly intimate union. In a marriage, sexual relations are a source of comfort, pleasure, and mutual support. But problems arise when sexual desire becomes an end in itself, overshadowing the total sharing of self which is the true purpose of sex. When sexual desire and physical fulfillment become paramount, the other person becomes a means to an end, an instrument for your own selfish pleasure. If pleasure is the only goal, there is little need for a true sharing of self.

The Habit of Fidelity

Fidelity is more than a physical reality. It is a state of mind, will, emotion, and heart. It is an intentional decision to save and share the best of ourselves for the relationships in which we invest the highest priority. Being faithful to our primary, prioritized relationships means making daily decisions to choose those relationships over the easy, the pleasurable, and the appealing. If we have prioritized our relationship with God, it means we decide to wake up early to make it to Sunday Mass, resisting the appeal of sleeping in or a leisurely brunch. If we prioritize our marital relationship, it means we take our spouse's interests and preferences into account before making decisions that affect us both. It means resisting the pleasurable feeling of being desired and the novelty of being with someone new. It means continuing to save the best of yourself (your time, your energy, your emotion) to share with your spouse rather than sharing your best with everyone else, leaving the dregs to the person you no longer feel a need to impress. Some married couples claim that the romance has gone out of their relationship. What they may be describing is not a lack of flowers and special dinners, but being taken for granted by someone who no longer feels the need to impress or even appreciate his or her partner.

Being faithful is a habit born of the conscious, intentional, daily decisions to keep the promises you have made. Like any habit, it takes time and practice to develop. Whatever your state in life, married or single, how can you practice fidelity?

One of the best ways to stay faithful is to avoid temptation. Placing yourself in situations where you know it will be difficult to keep your commitments sets yourself up for failures. When you decide to go on a diet, you don't set up a cot in the local ice cream shop. In fact, most nutritionists recommend that you clear your house of trigger foods—things that tempt you to overeat and lose discipline. The same idea applies here. If there are situations where you regularly find yourself tempted to break your promises, you need to find ways to avoid those situations. You may need to start meeting friends in coffee shops instead of bars or meet certain coworkers only in groups or in work situations. You may need to block websites that cause problems for you. The basic rule is always: Do what you can to make keeping promises easy and breaking promises difficult.

It's also important to respect the intimate relationships of others. Some single people see a married person as a safe outlet for confidences and flirting, precisely because the marriage would seem to preclude things going too far. In fact, the illusion of safety such relationships provide actually makes them more dangerous. It is important to keep appropriate boundaries around the intimate details of a relationship. It may seem exciting to go to the edge of what is acceptable with a person in a committed relationship, flirting, making suggestive comments, and the like. But even these "border attacks" can have a negative impact on the marital relationship, slowly eroding trust, making it more difficult for the spouses to share themselves fully with each other.

In the same way, a married friend may seem like the perfect confidant for discussing the problems in your marriage, providing the other gender's perspective. But sharing that is too intimate can violate the marriage bond, damaging the trust that lies at its heart. As a husband, it's fine to ask a female friend if she thinks your wife would prefer a bracelet or earrings as an anniversary gift. (No, she doesn't want a vacuum. Trust me.) It's not fine to share your concerns about your wife's recent decline in sexual interest. Intimate concerns should remain within the marriage when at all possible. If necessary, a medical professional or counselor might be consulted. Of course, if the health or safety of either partner is at stake, assistance must be sought as needed.

Cultivating the virtue of modesty can help to develop the habit of fidelity. Modesty seems old-fashioned, the province of the religious sects that live as in past centuries, wearing prairie dresses and bonnets. The *Catechism of the Catholic Church* explains the true nature of modesty: "[Modesty] means refusing to unveil what should remain hidden" (*CCC*, 2521). It goes on, "Modesty protects the mystery of persons and their love" (*CCC*, 2522). Though modesty should affect how we choose to dress, it must also affect how we behave. Quite simply, it means what belongs in a marriage should stay in the marriage. Barring issues of health and safety, couples should keep the intimate details of their relationship private. Those details are not fodder for blog posts, locker-room conversations, or reality shows.

Most people need to feel safe before sharing their true selves with another person. The sort of sharing that a good marriage requires means willingly giving another person weapons that can hurt you. Your spouse will know where your weaknesses are, your greatest fears and regrets. No one will ever share that information if they believe it will be used against them. Modesty guarantees that such information stays safely within the marriage. Oddly enough, keeping this information within the marriage actually strengthens the marriage. If another person can hurt you and refuses to do so, no matter the provocation, trust builds and it becomes easier and easier to share more deeply.

As we noted in our discussion of the third commandment, spending time together is an essential element of a healthy relationship. If you don't spend time together, there is little room for trust and sharing to grow. It's like planting a sequoia in a paper cup. It goes well for the first few weeks, but then either the cup tears or the roots wither. A weekly date night—even for just a walk around the neighborhood or a shared thermos of coffee in a park—can make an enormous differ-ence. As children arrive, it can become increasingly difficult to find time together since the absence of both parents requires coordination and a babysitter. A babysitting co-op, or well-synchronized sports practices, can help. Making an investment of time in the relationship, even when it's inconvenient, provides support for fidelity.

Finally, the habit of fidelity is fostered by selflessness. Selflessness means desiring the other's happiness more than your own, putting their needs ahead of your own. This way of living has a gotten a bad reputation, often because the selfless giving is not mutual. A marriage in which one partner loves selflessly while the other is selfish is a recipe for pain and often infidelity or breakdown. However, the solution is not for partners to see themselves as free agents, carefully weighing the situation and staying in the marriage only as long as they continue to see a net benefit. Instead, marriage calls both partners to love selflessly and forgive wholeheartedly. Paradoxically, the more both partners sacrifice for the common good, the more both will benefit and the stronger, the more loving, and the more faithful the marriage will grow.

Points to Remember

- The ninth commandment prohibits the forms of emotional infidelity that endanger relationships by damaging the trust at their base.
- Problems arise when sexual desire becomes an end in itself, overshadowing the total sharing of self which is the true purpose of sex.
- Fidelity is an intentional decision to save and share the best of ourselves for the relationships in which we invest the highest priority.
- The habit of fidelity is fostered by avoiding temptation, respecting the relationships of others, cultivating modesty, spending time together, and loving selflessly.

Culture Connection

Two films present the challenges of remaining emotionally faithful even in very difficult circumstances. Both *Iris* and *Away from Her* depict longstanding marriages that come to crisis when one spouse shows the onset of Alzheimer's disease. Though very difficult to watch, the stories of John and Iris and Grant and Fiona show the importance of building a strong base within marriage, of developing trust, and of shared responsibility for making decisions. When the marriage is strong, it survives the ravages of the disease, despite the inevitable pain.

Role Models: Marie-Azélie and Louis Martin

Marie-Azélie and Louis Martin are better known as the parents of St. Thérèse of Lisieux, but they are role models in their own right. Zélie was a successful lacemaker and Louis was a watchmaker, though he gave up his business to assist his wife when her business took off. Their lives had great difficulties. Four of their nine daughters died as infants or children. Marie-Azélie herself died of breast cancer when she was only forty-five and her youngest daughter (Thérèse) was only four. Louis lived for twelve more years.

As a couple, they were known for their great religious devotion and for the love that abounded in their family. Prayer and meditation were part of their daily lives and they shared their faith with their children. All of their surviving daughters entered religious life. Their surviving correspondence depicts a couple whose faith in God and in each other carried them through the joys and struggles of their lives.

Try This

For a week, spend a few minutes before bed thinking through your day and answering the following questions, writing your answers in a journal:

- What steps did I take to strengthen my priority relationships?
- What tempted me away from these relationships?
- What steps can I take to avoid or resist these temptations?

At the end of the week, do you notice that you are becoming more intentional about resisting temptation and strengthening your relationships? Were you able to identify any consistent problems that require more focused attention?

Talk It Through

- To what relationships am I called to be faithful?
- What cultural attitudes or circumstances make it most difficult to stay faithful?
- What can I change about how I live to develop the habit of fidelity?

Pray

God, you are always faithful.

Even when we wander far from you,

you never abandon us.

Help us learn to love with your selfless, forgiving heart

that we may remain faithful in our relationships.

Amen.

CHAPTER TEN

The Tenth Commandment
Bestowing Generosity

You shall not covet your neighbor's goods.

Need versus want. Financial planners will tell you that mastering that basic distinction is the foundation of financial security. Unfortunately, the advertising that surrounds us has one goal: to convince us that our wants are needs. A good ad can make us need something we don't even want. (Some physicians report that patients, having seen repeated pharmaceutical ads, request treatment for diseases they don't have.) When we begin to confuse wants with needs, we are constantly tempted to indulge and to overspend. We may find ourselves trapped in a cycle of spending and debt, making our happiness dependent on acquiring more possessions and the "right" possessions.

It's worth asking the question: Do we own our possessions or do they own us? When acquiring possessions becomes the priority, it begins to drain our time, energy, and resources. We spend our time looking for ways to get the things we want or maintaining and using the things we have. The possibility of losing what we have or of not being able to get everything we want becomes a source of anxiety and, sometimes, depression. Our energy goes into keeping up appearances rather than building solid relationships with God, self, and others. Our self-worth is not based on our dignity as a child of God, but on a number at the bottom of a balance sheet.

An unbalanced relationship with things can have a negative impact on our relationship with others. Do we see what others have and embrace their good fortune or wonder why our luck has not been as good? Making the acquisition of things our priority places us squarely on the path to wanting what others have and becoming jealous or resenting them for having what we want but do not possess.

In addition, the desire for wealth and possessions is often tied to a desire for power. It's painfully clear to anyone who is paying attention that power and wealth are closely linked in modern society. The people who hold political offices are typically among the most advantaged members of society. Even more significant, in many cases, the people who exercise power *behind* the scenes are among the wealthiest in the nation. Now, there's nothing particularly wrong with the richer people in a country taking leading roles in government, industry, and other institutions. In some laudable cases, privileged families educate their children to take positions that allow them to give back to the community rather than living in indolent luxury. Many wealthy people are exceptionally generous with their wealth, improving the lives of thousands immeasurably. In less laudable instances, wealthy individuals seek political and economic power so that they can structure the system to their own benefit, increasing their wealth to others' detriment.

The final commandment addresses unbalanced relationships with things by addressing the desire that underlies envy, greed, and acquisitiveness. Moving past our desire to have more to a desire to share more is a critical final step in developing right relationships. It helps to ensure that our priorities have penetrated every aspect of our lives and we are willing to do all that is necessary to keep these priorities in proper perspective.

Trust and Providence

When we discussed the seventh commandment, we saw that possessions didn't seem to mean much to Jesus. In his preaching, Jesus praised the poor because they relied so completely on God. They trusted in God, often because they had nowhere else to turn. Jesus holds out their trust in God as a model to all the faithful, promising his followers that where their treasure was their heart would be. If God is your treasure, your heart will rest in him. However, if you trust in your possessions, your heart will seek its comfort in cold cash and shiny trinkets. Some people follow the model Jesus proposed in a very literal way, giving away everything they possess and taking a vow of poverty, owning nothing throughout their lives, living in solidarity with the poor. Most of us will not feel called to such a dramatic change in our lifestyles. But we can give serious consideration to where we place our trust. Do we trust in God or in our material possessions?

The tenth commandment calls us to rely on God's providence. *Providence* means that we trust that God will provide for all our needs. Now, reliance on God's providence doesn't mean that you can empty your checking account to pay for a month-long luxury cruise, trusting that God will pay your electric bill when you get back. Instead, trusting in God allows you to give generously of your resources, knowing that God will not abandon you.

Obeying the tenth commandment requires that we develop the habit of generosity. Generosity relies on detachment. Detachment is the ability to let go of our possessions. Detachment requires that you have the appropriate relationship with yourself, understanding that you are valuable because you are a child of God, no matter your wealth or status. When we are attached to the things we own, measuring our self-worth by our possessions, giving away the things we own is very difficult. It seems like giving away a piece of our identity. We hang on as tightly as we can, no matter how great the need. It's like we revert to the pesky toddler stage when the only word that mattered was "Mine!" Toy, mine! Cookie, mine! Doggie, mine! Grass, mine! This attitude is not a hallmark of spiritual maturity. On the other hand, detachment allows us to give generously. Things are just things. It doesn't matter who owns them. If someone has a greater need, detachment makes it easier to give away what you have to meet that need.

Almsgiving is a traditional practice of faith, attested as far back as Abraham who gave the priest Melchizedek a tenth of the treasure he captured in battle. In the book of Tobit, the archangel Raphael speaks of the importance of giving alms:

> Prayer with fasting is good. Almsgiving with righteousness is
> better than wealth with wickedness. It is better to give alms
> than to store up gold, for almsgiving saves from death, and

purges all sin. Those who give alms will enjoy a full life, but those who commit sin and do evil are their own worst enemies (Tobit 12:8–10).

Almsgiving, along with fasting and prayer, is one of the Church's penitential disciplines, helping us to learn detachment, letting go of the things of this world so as to cling ever more tightly to God. Though often related to the observance of Lent, the practices of prayer, fasting, and almsgiving are valuable throughout the year.

As the seventh and tenth commandments are related, both addressing our relationship with things, it's not surprising that fasting and almsgiving are closely related as well. In fasting, we give up food or other things for a specified period of time. As we move from gratitude to generosity, we may decide to use the money we save from our fast as alms, given to those whose need is greater.

Seeking Detachment

So, what practical steps can we take to develop this detachment and become more generous in our almsgiving?

Becoming more generous starts with taking a serious look at how you deal with your money and your time. The easiest way to do this is to look at your spending, particularly how much time and money you spend on luxuries and extras compared to how much you give away. If you spend twice as much money on music downloads or designer coffee than you do on charitable donations, you may have an imbalance. Similarly, if you spend more time at the movies or playing video games than you do donating your time, you may have an imbalance.

Once you know how much time and money you spend and how much you give away, you are ready to take the next step. You need to decide what portion of your income you want to give away. That's not as easy a question as you might think. Ultimately, it will be a very personal choice, determined, at least in part, by your other expenses. A family with several children in parochial school facing significant health expenses will likely have a lower number than a single person with a large discretionary income.

The tenth commandment invites us to give as much as we can of both our time and our treasure. How much we give of each may change over time. When I was in graduate school, I lived on almost no money and a fairly steady diet of yogurt and rice cakes. Clearly, there wasn't a lot of discretionary money to give away, but I did have a very flexible schedule, so I gave as much of my time as I could.

Until they see the stark numbers, most people think that they are far more generous than they are. You may think you are giving away ten percent of your net income when, in fact, your contributions total just two percent. The same goes for how you spend your time. If you are as generous as you want to be, you're done. If you want to be more generous, you will need to look back at the accounting that began this exercise to decide where you can free up money or time to help others. Starting by giving up the little extras will help us develop the detachment that allows us to grow in reliance on God. As we become accustomed to giving of ourselves, detachment becomes easier and easier. The good that we do with our time and money will take precedence over the comfort, passing pleasure, and security that time and money might otherwise provide.

Of course, once you have decided how much you want to give away, you must decide who will get it—another personal choice. Some people decide to make large gifts of time or money to a single cause. For example, you may decide to volunteer ten hours of time a month, spending all of that time assisting at a local crisis pregnancy center. Others decide to give smaller amounts of time or money to several causes. In that case, the ten hours might be spent serving meals at a homeless shelter, reading aloud to children at the public library, and helping to clean and decorate the church sanctuary. In donating time and money, some people focus on a single cause, perhaps religion or health care or education. Others spread their donations across several causes. All of those options are laudable. Do what works for you. (Please just don't convince yourself that going to a benefit concert by your favorite singer is a charitable donation!)

A key element in any donation you make is to ensure that the money or time is used well. As a volunteer, you want to make sure that you are engaged in tasks that need to be done, no matter how humble. Peeling potatoes to make lunch at a homeless shelter is likely to be far more useful than sitting in an office attending a phone that never rings. For monetary donations, many agencies and websites show how charities use the donations they receive, evaluating the efficiency and effectiveness of the use.

As with most things, practice makes perfect. The very act of giving helps us to develop detachment. We realize that our lives are far richer when we are giving of ourselves and so, giving even more becomes easier. Our possessions are no longer our primary sources of joy and security. Being generous teaches us to rely on God above all else.

Points to Remember

- An inordinate desire for wealth and possessions, particularly envy for what others have, is a sign of an unbalanced relationship with things.
- Instead of relying on worldly goods, the tenth commandment calls us to place our trust solely in God who will give us all we need.
- The habit of generosity requires that we develop detachment, recognizing that our value as individuals comes from the dignity with which God has gifted us, not from what we own.

Culture Connection

The movie *Clueless* may seem like a strange choice to illustrate a commandment about not coveting goods. After all, it's the story of a group of extremely spoiled teenagers who get everything they want and who judge each other based on the clothes they wear, the cars they drive, and the gadgets they possess. But the real story of the film is Cher's growth from a shallow rich girl to a young woman who looks beneath the surface to find the good in the people around her, who begins to attend to people's true needs. Ultimately, she learns to give back and become part of something bigger than the next hot fashion trend.

Role Model (and Role Model—Not!): The Poor Widow and Ananias and Sapphira

[Jesus] sat down opposite the treasury and observed how the crowd put money into the treasury. Many rich people put in large sums. A poor widow also came and put in two small coins worth a few cents. Calling his disciples to himself, he

said to them, "Amen, I say to you, this poor widow put in more
than all the other contributors to the treasury. For they have
all contributed from their surplus wealth, but she, from her
poverty, has contributed all she had, her whole livelihood."
(Mark 12:41–44)

Clearly, this widow knew something of generosity. She didn't give
much, but she gave what she had. God didn't get her leftovers—he got
the best she had to offer.

On the other hand, the Acts of the Apostles (5:1–11) tells the story
of Ananias and Sapphira. You know the old saying, "If you can't be a
good example, at least be a horrible warning!" Well, this husband and
wife greed team are certainly that warning for us. The early Church
was marked by its members bringing to the apostles their money or
the proceeds from selling their property to be shared with those in
need. Ananias and Sapphira wanted to join the company of donors,
but there was a catch. They wanted to earn praise for their generosity,
but they didn't want to give away *everything* they got for selling a piece
of land. So, they tucked away part of the proceeds and donated the
rest—claiming that they had given the complete proceeds. Confronted
with their lies and their greed (for money and for praise), Ananias and
Sapphira literally dropped dead. Now *that's* a horrible warning!

Try This

For a week, spend a few minutes before bed thinking through your
day and answering the following questions, writing your answers in a
journal:

- Was I asked to buy anything today? How did I respond?
- Was I asked to give anything (money, possession, time) away today? How did I respond?

At the end of the week, look over the reflections to see if there is a pattern in your responses. Do you respond to requests to give or to buy differently? If so, why do you respond this way? How do you feel about your responses?

Talk It Through

- When I am shopping, how do I decide whether I need something or whether I want something?
- How do I feel about money? Does it mean luxury? Pleasure? Security? Possibilities?
- How do I decide how much of my time and money I will donate and to whom?

Pray

Lord,

you give us all we need.

Help us to trust in your loving care

and share what we have generously

with our brothers and sisters,

especially those in greatest need.

Amen.

What's Next?

Learning to live in right relationship with God, self, others, and things is not like a weekend remodeling project—a bout of intensive effort with a clear ending (in my case, typically followed by a hot bath, a glass of wine, and a good novel). Instead, living in these relationships is a lifelong path that leads to an ultimate destination: eternal life with God.

On a long road trip, it's not uncommon to be seduced off the prescribed route in search of a shortcut or a bypass around traffic or construction. All too often, those shortcuts save us neither time nor stress as we wander through unfamiliar territory trying to find our way. (And they always seem to leave me somewhere in New Hampshire. I live in Maryland.) In the same way, in life, we are often seduced away from the right relationships we try to maintain by actions or opportunities that promise greater ease or pleasure. Frequently, these detours take us farther and farther away from our ultimate goal, miring us in confusion and lack of balance. In such cases, the Ten Commandments are our GPS, helping us recalculate our route and regain the balanced relationships we desire.

All for One and One for All

Looking back over the previous chapters, it's pretty obvious that the Ten Commandments are closely related to each other. They don't exist in ten hermetically sealed vacuums. The more faithfully you follow each commandment, the easier following the others becomes. As the *Catechism of the Catholic Church* states:

> The Decalogue [the Ten Commandments—*Decalogue* means "ten words"] forms a coherent whole. Each "word" refers to each of the others and to all of them; they reciprocally condition one another. The two tablets shed light on one another; they form an organic unity. To transgress one commandment is to infringe all the others (cf. James 2:10–11). One cannot honor another person without blessing God his Creator. One cannot adore God without loving all men, his creatures. The Decalogue brings man's religious and social life into unity. (*CCC*, 2069)

Putting your relationships in order is a process that gathers momentum. The more time you spend on your relationship with God, the closer that relationship will become. The closer your relationship with God, the more deeply you will feel his love. This love allows you to understand yourself as a precious child of God, conformed to Christ by the sacrament of baptism. Secure in this knowledge, it becomes much easier to love the people around you. Understanding yourself as a child of God makes it very difficult to deny the humanity of the people with whom you come in contact. Living in authentic, loving relationships puts things in their right place. There is no need to acquire more and more to salve the human longing for connection. You don't need to use things to draw people to you. On the other hand, without a balanced relationship with God and with self, it becomes all too tempting to use other people, possessions, and power to make you feel worthy, valuable, and loved.

As we've seen repeatedly, living the commandments requires more than just avoiding evil. Most of us will never consider stealing or intentionally injuring someone, let alone killing someone. If various studies are to be believed, most people will never commit adultery. The greater challenge for most of us is making consistent daily choices to go the extra mile and do the right thing. Over time, making these choices will build habits. As we choose to follow the commandments, we make God our priority, spending the time needed to develop an intimate relationship with him. We become respectful, grateful, honest, faithful, and generous people who live with integrity, honoring the dignity of everyone we meet. Developing any one of these habits makes acquiring the others easier. The good habits engendered by following the commandments reinforce each other. Being a person who lives with integrity makes it more likely that you'll be honest. To do otherwise would create an internal conflict. Similarly, you can't respect people and uphold their dignity while being unfaithful or treating them as instruments for your pleasure.

Unfortunately, it works the other way as well. Abandoning one habit threatens all the others. People who don't receive God's gifts with gratitude are rarely generous. They have earned what they have. Why share it with others who have not made the effort to earn life's good things? If you don't make it a priority to take the time to create an intimate relationship—with God or another person—what difference will it make whether you keep your promises? It's much easier to betray someone you don't really know. Now, one mistake doesn't lead you on to a path of no return, making it useless to even try to be good. But repeatedly violating the commandments, instead of following them, can create bad habits that are very hard to break.

Signposts Back to the Path

So, when we make mistakes, how do we nip them in the bud, before they have time to grow into a full-blown bad habit? What practical steps can we take to redirect us to the path designated by the commandments?

If you've been following the journaling exercises at the end of each chapter, you've already taken a first step. These journaling exercises have helped you reflect on your life in a serious, spiritual way. Writing your reflections down in a journal is a way of allowing yourself to go back and look for patterns or growth over time. In the craziness of life with its deadlines and to-do lists and errands and chores, it's hard to learn to take the time to quiet your mind and reflect. The quiet time we get in our days (if there is any) is usually spent planning for the days ahead or simply allowing the mind to drift. Practicing the discipline of daily prayerful reflection is a great way to make sure that you stay on the right path. Think of it as regularly checking the map to make sure you're still going the right way. (Unfortunately, life rarely comes with a voice saying "Recalculate" to let us know we've wandered from our path.)

This daily reflection lays the foundation for a regular examination of conscience. The purpose of an examination of conscience isn't to beat yourself up about all the ways you've failed. Instead, it helps you ensure that bad habits don't develop and to identify the detours that keep drawing you away from God. It keeps you honest with yourself and with God.

A regular examination of conscience will lead you to a regular celebration of the sacrament of reconciliation. This underutilized sacrament is a celebration of God's loving forgiveness, a ritual reminder that, no matter how far or how often we stray, God is always waiting, with joy, to welcome us back to the path. Celebrating this sacrament regularly requires the deep sharing that increases the intimacy of our relationship with God. To continue the travel metaphor, think of it as regular maintenance for the car.

Finally, regular reception of the Eucharist is crucial. You'd never leave for a long road trip without gas. Why would you travel on your spiritual path without fuel for that journey? Celebrating the eucharistic liturgy draws us closer to God and to our brothers and sisters in Christ. Hearing the Word of God proclaimed and receiving the Eucharist strengthens us to stay the course, making good choices to obey the commandments and develop the habits that will keep our relationships balanced and filled with love.

Points to Remember

- Living in right relationships is a lifelong path that leads to an ultimate destination: eternal life with God.

- Living the commandments is a cumulative process. The more good we do, the easier it becomes to do good. Following one commandment makes it easier to follow them all.
- Tools to stay on the right path include daily reflection, examination of conscience, and the sacraments of Eucharist and penance.

Try This

For a week, spend a few minutes before bed thinking through your day and answering the following questions, writing your answers in a journal:

- What parts of your life felt out of balance today?
- What steps did you take to reestablish the balance?
- How successful were you in restoring the balance?

At the end of the week, review all the entries and see what patterns become obvious. Are there specific relationships that you struggle to keep in balance? Have you gotten better at restoring the balance when necessary?

Talk It Through

- Are there particular detours that tempt you away from where you want to go? What about these detours are so appealing?
- What signs tell you that you are on the wrong path? How do you realign your path when you have drifted away?
- Has your study of the Ten Commandments helped you to refocus your spiritual life? What practices have you identified to help you continue on this path? What accountability have you created to ensure that these practices will remain part of your life?

Pr ay

Lord,

our goal is to live with you forever.

Help us to always seek

the path that will lead to you.

When we stray from that path,

remind us that you wait with love

to lead us back to you.

Amen.